RIDDLES
and the 9Fs

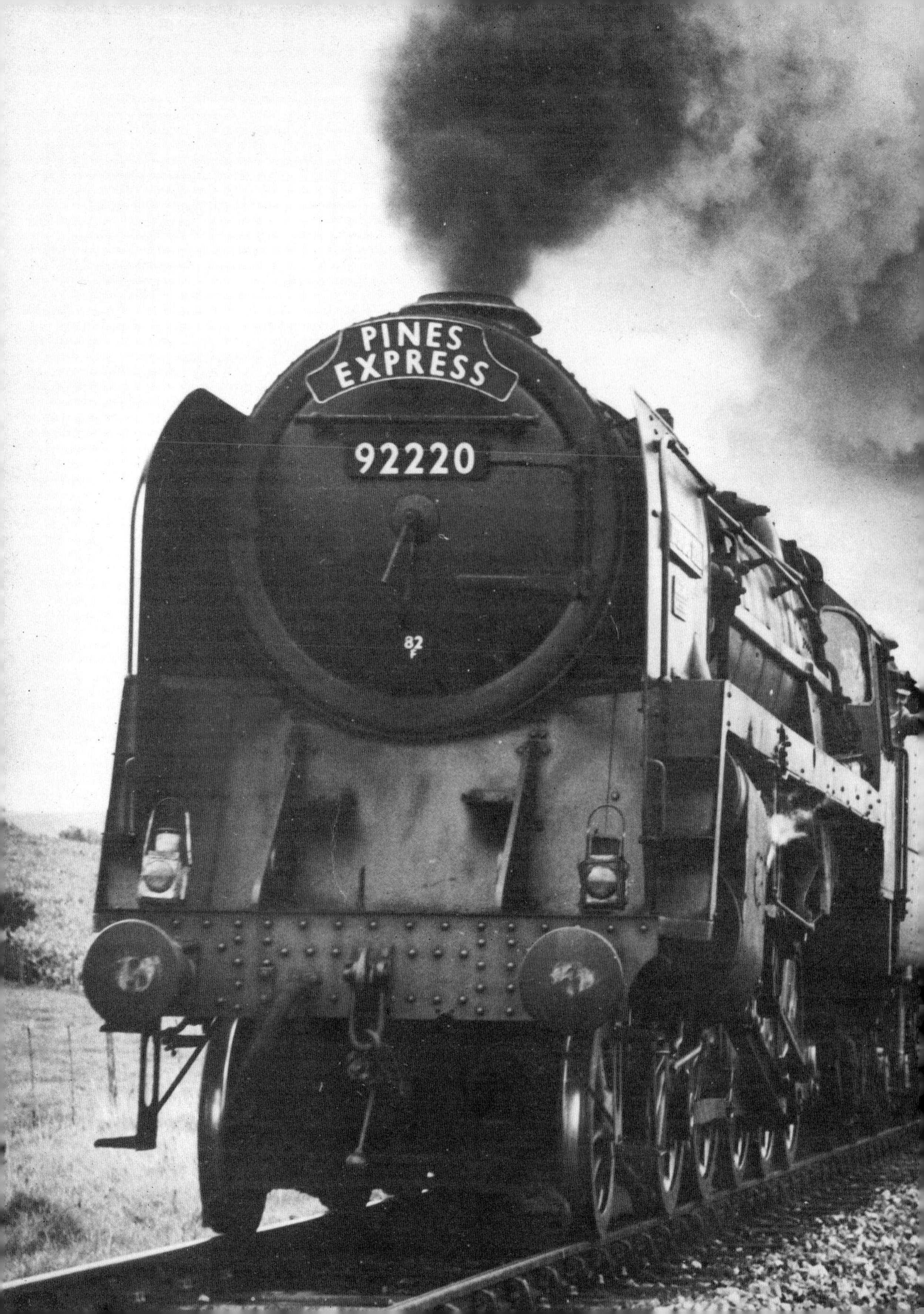
PINES
EXPRESS
92220
82F

RIDDLES
and the 9Fs

Colonel H.C.B. Rogers OBE

LONDON

IAN ALLAN LTD

First published 1982

ISBN 0 7110 1208 3

Published by Ian Allan Ltd, Shepperton, Surrey;
and printed by Ian Allan Printing Ltd at their works
at Coombelands in Runnymede, England

To My Wife
who treasures her friendship
with
Robin and Irene Riddles

Contents

Acknowledgements

In the writing of this book I have been indebted chiefly to
the designer of the '9F' class freight locomotives himself,
my friend Mr R. A. Riddles, CBE, FIMechE, who has
read and commented on every chapter. Another friend,
the late Mr R. C. Bond FICE, FIMechE, supplied me
with valuable information up till the time of his sudden
death. Mr P. N. Townend, FIMechE, Traction and
Maintenance Engineer British Railways Eastern Region,
and Mr T. A. Greaves, FIMechE, Traction and Train
Crew Manager British Railways, have been most
generous in the help they have given me, both in the
provision of photographs and accounts of the '9Fs' in
service. That eminent railway enthusiast Mr D. S. M.
Barrie, OBE FCIT, responded readily to my request for
help. Col K. R. M. Cameron, FIMechE, has provided me
with delightful photographs and reminiscences of the
'Austerity' 2-10-0s in the Middle East. I owe my
information on '9Fs' on the Southern Region to Mr S. C.
Townroe, FIMechE. Mr R. G. Jarvis, FIMechE, has told
me much about the construction of the '9F' locomotives.
Finally, Mr D. R. Carling. M A, FIMechE, and one-time
Superintending Engineer of the Locomotive Testing
Station at Rugby has given me details of tests carried out
on variously modified '9F' 2-10-0s.

1
R. A. Riddles, CBE

It is pertinent that a book about a steam locomotive, which was probably one of the most outstanding ever to run in the British Isles, should start with a brief account of the designer's career, with emphasis on those aspects of it which may have influenced his own ideas and practice.

Robert Arthur Riddles ('Robin' to his close friends and relations) was born in 1892, and in 1909, at the age of 17, he joined the London & North Western Railway Company as a premium apprentice at its Crewe Locomotive Works. Crewe, the most famous locomotive works in the country — perhaps in the world — owed some of its prestige to being builder of locomotives for the Premier Line, the proud badge of which was the figure of Britannia, armed with trident and shield, and surrounded by such a wealth of gold ornamentation, that its appearance on the splashers of F. W. Webb's 0-6-0 express goods engines earned them the nickname of 'Cauliflowers'!

Of his arrival at Crewe, Riddles says: 'There was I, landed at Crewe, further away from home than I had ever been, working from 6am till 5.45pm, $9\frac{3}{4}$ hours of actual work for the princely sum of four shillings per week; and this was followed by evening classes at the Mechanics Institution from 7 till 9 o'clock each evening except Saturday. Yet I enjoyed the work and often felt sorry that it was time to go home.' This enthusiasm and capacity for hard work were to last him throughout his career.

His first original piece of research related to locomotive chimneys. He says: 'The old North Western chimneys were made of sheet steel, except for the top. I noticed that the centre part always had holes worn near the top, where a strip of steel $1\frac{1}{2}$in by $\frac{1}{4}$in was riveted round the inside, and I set to work to find out why this ring had been put in. Without it no repairs would have been necessary because it was at this point that the steel plate corroded. The man who put the ring in did not know its purpose, nor did the Chief Draughtsman, and for a long time I could find no explanation. Then at last I came across an old man who told me that it was a water ring. This was interesting, but I could not think what on earth it could have to do with water. Eventually an old driver who had served under Ramsbottom provided the solution. He said that in Ramsbottom's day, when engines were really clean, the priming of the engine resulted in water being carried up the chimney and all over the boiler barrel covering, making an awful mess. The drivers found that by putting a worn piston ring inside the chimney the water was thrown back into the smokebox. The "water ring" therefore became official. It was a small triumph that as a result of my investigations these rings were shortly abandoned.'

It was this quality of observation, combined with a refusal to accept anything without an adequate reason, which played no small part in Riddles's rise to the summit of his profession.

A minor point of interest in the above story is that one is accustomed to regard the years preceding 1914 as those in which London & North Western engines were immaculately turned out; yet here was an old driver harking back to the years before 1870 when 'engines were really clean'!

As Riddles passed through the shops his interest and keenness increased. In after life he realised how much he had been indebted to the wisdom of men who had spent their lives in locomotive shops. there was, for instance, the old charge hand for new building who had supervised the erection of more than 1,000 locomotives. To him Riddles remarked one day that the managers must be very clever men. 'You get the job, Mr Riddles,' he replied, 'and you will have dozens to show you how to do it.' Riddles comments, 'How true; but how difficult to determine which of the dozens is right; and in this, as I subsequently found, lies the lonely responsibility of decision.'

The LNWR engines did a magnificent job, but they were very cheaply constructed and consequently needed much maintenance. Riddles says: 'The frame plates were too thin in section and had to be continually welded up; strengthening plates had to be put over the horn blocks; and with the heavy and cumbersome Joy's valve gear it was impossible to get constant lead in the valve opening in all positions of the reversing gear, and fractures of the motion were frequent. It was only when initial inspection was introduced that flaws were discovered and failures reduced. But whatever the merits or demerits of the stud, they would haul 420ton out of Euston, sparks flying to high heaven, and many times during the periods of holiday traffic I have watched trains arrive at Crewe from London and heard the shed "turner" say to the driver, "Is he all right, Mate?" On getting the affirmative, the tender would be coaled from a wagon alongside in Crewe station, and off she would go to Liverpool, Manchester, Holyhead or Carlisle. The Drawing Office, as I knew it, "went cheap", and there was little in the way of failures to guide them. It was the good work of drivers, firemen, and shed staff, combined with North Western pride, that produced the results, despite the defects in the tools which they were given.'

In 1910 the exchange trials took place during which the LNWR 'Experiment' class 4-6-0 No 1471 *Worcestershire* ran Great Western trains from Paddington and a GWR 'Star' class 4-6-0 No 4005 *Polar Star*, came to the

LNWR to haul trains over the West Coast route; both engines being at that time unsuperheated. The Great Western engine impressed Riddles. He wrote: 'The trial with *Polar Star* took place whilst I was at Crewe, and I saw this beautiful engine come into the station — the paint immaculate, the motion beautifully machined, and the footplate fittings polished. The engine not only *looked* good, it *was* good. Bowen Cooke had to do something and designs for the "Claughton" class were developed. But there seemed to be the same old outlook and the same old questions were asked: "What parts can we use that we have patterns for? How shall we make the boiler, using as many of the existing press blocks as possible?" The result was a lost opportunity, for the boiler was much too small and inefficient. Even when a new and bigger boiler was fitted in later years, it never matched up to the job, which depended, as before, on the skill of the driver and the hard work of the fireman for its achievement.' The young Riddles who admired *Polar Star* can hardly have imagined that in time to come the lines of his own engines would reflect so clearly their descent from those of G. J. Churchward.

Superheating was adopted widely on both railways within a very short time; but Churchward chose a much lower degree of superheat than did Bowen Cooke, but the brilliant Great Western locomotive engineer has been much criticised in consequence. Nevertheless, at that time oils had not been developed sufficiently to withstand very high temperatures. The LNWR superheated locomotives worked at a steam temperature of 650°F, as compared with the approximate 550°F of the GWR. In a letter to the author, Riddles writes that he first encountered superheating in the 'Princes' and 'Georges' during his apprenticeship. He adds: 'I remember the trouble we had with carbonisation in the early days, with valve rings being seized up etc, and valves having to be driven out of the valve chambers with lead hammers. Snifting valves were fitted, to open when coasting; but, as the oil quality improved, they were abandoned because they created other problems and had become unnecessary.' Riddles believes that Churchward, realising the likelihood of the oil carbonising, and having the advantage of superior Welsh coal, wisely pursued a cautious policy. 'In any case', he says, 'the Great Western locomotives were far and away better than most, so why invite trouble? The real culprits were his successors who should have realised the benefits of higher superheat, with the advent of improved oils.'

Riddles' first footplate experience was in 1911 when all the 'premiums' and pupils were asked to volunteer for work during the strike of that year. He was detailed to fire a 'Precedent' class 2-4-0 rostered to fetch the District Engineer into Crewe — a light engine only, but he says that 'it rolled and rocketed about and I had great difficulty in getting my coal through the fire hole door at all. The District Engineer remarked: "You haven't been doing much of this?" "No Sir," I replied. "I thought not".'

When in August 1914 war broke out, Riddles was in the Erecting Shop at Rugby, and he obtained permission to follow the example of many of his friends and join the Army. It was not long before Sapper Riddles of the Royal

Engineers was in France, where he spent most of the war with an Engineer Field Company of the Guards Division. Before the end of the war he had been given a commission in the Royal Engineers and had been badly wounded. When he eventually left the Army he had a wife but no job. He wrote to Bowen Cooke, CME of the LNWR, who replied that his old job in the Erecting Shop at Rugby was still open to him; and so Riddles returned to Rugby as a fitter — a somewhat lowly position for an ex-officer. In those days a fitter had his own engine to strip and reassemble, and the assistance of a mate. Riddles' mate had been a Priveleged Apprentice before the war and during it had reached the rank of captain in The Oxford-shire & Buckinghamshire Light Infantry. When the 1919 strike brought the railway to a stop, the two of them volunteered for driving and firing and were given the 'turn' for the Holyhead 'Irish Mail' from Rugby. They took the engine out of the shed and were waiting for the signal, when to their relief they were told that the strike was over and that the regular crew had arrived. They were both 'sent to Coventry', which they did not mind much. However, they had not heard the last of their action during the strike, for they were summoned before a Union branch meeting to explain their conduct. Riddles let fly at them, saying that he had been in France whilst they were striking for more pay and his mates were being killed for lack of ammunition. He told the Committee it could do what the hell it liked, and left. They wrote to H. P. M. Beames, the Works Manager, asking to be transferred to Crewe. Beames agreed and posted them to the Mill-wrights' Shop.

Riddles was not left in a subordinate positioned for long because Beames had recognised his ability and on 25 November 1919 he placed him in charge of a project for the construction of a pre-fabricated housing estate to provide dwellings for LNWR employees who were suffer-ing from a housing shortage in Crewe. He had some qualification for the task because after he had been wounded and graded as unfit for active service he had been posted to a Works Company on Salisbury Plain and placed in command of a detachment of sappers and a mass of German prisoners of war engaged in constructing various military buildings.

Beames was so impressed with the way that he had tackled the housing estate that, even before he had finished, he gave him the additional task of building the new Erecting Shop, Steel Works. Riddles was now a marked man and was soon serving as a technical member on various investigation and economy committees. Beames had succeeded to the appointment of CME on the death of Bowen Cooke, and on 15 December 1920 he put Riddles in charge of all locomotive and associated build-ing, with responsibility to the CME under whom all such buildings came. A week later he was appointed Assistant to Works Manager — a rapid rise for the defiant fitter of just over a year before.

In 1922 the London & North Western and the Lanca-shire & Yorkshire Railways were amalgamated. George Hughes, CME of the latter, was senior by appointment to Beames and so became CME of what was the enlarged LNWR.

An early but important step by Hughes was to direct that LNWR engines should be fitted with Belpaire boilers in replacement of the existing round-topped variety, because of the small volume allowed by the latter for the disengagement of steam. It was another stage in the as yet unresolved argument as to the respective merits of the two types.

After the amalgamation responsibility for outside buildings was transferred to the District Engineers, which made Riddles redundant; but he was soon placed in charge of the recording office at Crewe, known as the Progress Office.

It was not long after this amalgamation that the fusion took place of the independent railway companies, and on 1 January 1923 the enlarged LNWR became part of the London Midland & Scottish Railway, with George Hughes as CME and Sir Henry Fowler of the Midland Railway as his Deputy. Beames remained as Mechanical Engineer for the area of the enlarged LNWR. Riddles was sent to Horwich for a month to study the method adopted there for the initial inspection of locomotives coming in for repair. The Horwich system was very good and Riddles returned to develop it at Crewe, where, despite strong initial opposition from Beames, it was successfully introduced with far-reaching results.

The disastrous General Strike occurred in 1926. Riddles undertook to drive and was given *Edith Cavell*, a 'Prince of Wales' class 4-6-0 engine built in 1915. He says: 'After a 30-hour standstill on the line, I took the first train from Crewe into Manchester, and did two round trips a day for the next two days. On the second day I set up a record from Manchester to Crewe; stopping at every station (13 of them) and doing the journey of 31 miles in under the hour — a feat which was noted by the Press. On the third day I was given a "George the Fifth" and I could not obtain anything like the acceleration and had difficulty in stopping the engine from slipping; though once under way it ran like a hare. On the fourth day I asked for *Edith* again, and was booked to run from Crewe to Carlisle on the "Scotch Express"!'

Having some difficulty in climbing Grayrigg (a longer pull than Shap, though not so steep), he thought Shap would present even more of a problem, particularly with a 'green' driver, and so refused to start from Tebay until he had a full head of steam and a full fire. When they did get going he had to take a turn with the shovel himself, because the 'Princes' and 'Experiments', with their long and level grates, were not the easiest to fire. As it was, they made a very fast ascent of Shap, but arrived at Penrith with no steam left at all and little water!

The practical experience as a driver during this period impressed him with the value of adhesion given by additional coupled wheels. It was an impression which lasted throughout his career in the railway service and which played no small part in his insistence on 10-coupled wheels for a heavy freight locomotive. He maintains that the practical knowledge acquired by driving an engine is invaluable to anyone who has to take major decisions on design. *Edith Cavell*, therefore, has an important niche in locomotive history as the progenitor in part of the '9F' class 2-10-0. Appropriately, one of the engine's name-plates, lined out by Riddles in the old LNWR livery, is secured to the wall of his sun lounge.

Owing to Riddles' outstanding ability, his rise on the LMS was rapid. The story of that rise has been told in another book[1] so that only those parts which have some relevance to the development of his own ideas on steam locomotive design are repeated here.

The LMS, having decided to reorganise Crewe Works, Riddles was put in charge of the job as Clerk of the Works. He achieved such excellent results that in 1928 he was appointed Assistant Works Superintendent Derby. Before he left Crewe, Beames had become enthusiastic about Caprotti valves, and he had Riddles fitting them to some of the four-cylinder 'Claughton' class 4-6-0s. Riddles was himself impressed with the Caprotti gear, and regarded poppet valves, after they had been suitably developed, as the ideal for the steam locomotives of the future; but he considers that Beames should have tried them first on small engines. The 'Claughtons' were the London & North Western's latest and biggest express engines, so that attention was drawn to the inevitable 'teething' troubles. Later, 20 'Claughtons' were given a much bigger boiler and results had been sufficiently satisfactory for some of them to be given the Caprotti valve gear.

Riddles' new chief, the Works Superintendent Derby, was H. G. Ivatt, a fellow London & North Western man who had arrived at Crewe as an apprentice about five years before Riddles. He had a very tranquil disposition and told his Assistant to ease up as he was not at Crewe; 'And', says Riddles, 'brought me down to earth from the rush and bustle to which I had become accustomed. Indeed, at Crewe, I had acquired the nicknames of "Blood out of a Stone" and "Ninety Minutes to the Hour"!'

Before Riddles arrived at Derby the LMS had placed an order with the North British Locomotive Company for 50 three-cylinder express passenger engines, and all of these, the 'Royal Scot' class, were in service by the end of the year. Another batch of 20 was ordered in 1930, but these engines were built at Derby Works under the supervision of Ivatt and Riddles. The 'Claughtons' with the bigger boiler had shown such an improvement after receiving it, that it was decided to make them still better by a much more radical reconstruction. In 1930, therefore, two of them were rebuilt with this boiler but with a three-cylinder chassis like the 'Royal Scots'. They were so good that their performance was very little inferior to that of the 'Royal Scots'; and 20 more completely new engines were built to this design soon after Stanier's arrival and incorporating some of his ideas. Nominally they were 'Claughton' rebuilds, but it is unlikely that anything more than the wheel centres were taken from the engines they replaced. Almost inevitably they were nicknamed 'Baby Scots'.

In October 1930 Sir Henry Fowler was replaced as CME by E. J. H. Lemon, though the latter's appointment was temporary. In 1931 Lemon posted Riddles back to Crewe as Assistant Works Superintendent to his namesake, F. A. Lemon. In January of the following year W. A. Stanier, from the Great Western Railway, was appointed CME of the London Midland & Scottish Railway, and E. J. H. Lemon became a Vice-President.

In order to get everybody working together, Stanier was anxious that the design and building of his new range of locomotives should go ahead as quickly as possible, and he was determined that they should not resemble those of the London & North Western, Midland, or any other pre-Grouping constituent of the company, but should have a new and distinctive LMS appearance. In this he was successful, but the taper boiler and shape of the firebox hinted strongly of Great Western ancestry! Many Swindon practices were indeed adopted not only in the design of the engines, but, more particularly, in the workshops, where the equipment installed was far more elaborate and expensive than had ever previously been used at Crewe. Stanier had been rather horrified at Crewe's traditional way of doing things on the cheap and producing engine fittings 'as cast' — a tradition which went back to the days of Ramsbottom.

The most important LMS locomotive requirement was for an express engine, more powerful than the 'Royal Scots', which would be able to work trains through between Euston and Glasgow, a distance of over 400 miles, without an intermediate stop. Wanting a wide firebox, Stanier decided on a Pacific (perhaps with memories of the GWR *Great Bear*), and the result was the apppearance in 1933 of the first of a new class, the four-cylinder 4-6-2 *Princess Royal*. This, and a sister engine, were built at Crewe under the immediate super-vision of Riddles. He and his men worked literally day and night in the shops to get the engine ready in time to be at Euston on the date fixed for its inspection by the Directors. The boiler was by far the biggest ever built at Crewe, and of the many problems which arose one which was particularly difficult to solve was the application of the boiler clothing. The old LNWR boiler covering, to which Crewe was accustomed was a poor quality felt, which was whitewashed on one side, and which after a short time was completely scorched away between the lagging bands. However, 'still air', says Riddles, 'is a very fine insulator'; and the LNWR lagging, or lack of it, indicated that, if the need arose, lagging could be omitted provided that the space between the boiler and the lagging plates was airtight. He made use of this attribute when he came to design his 'Austerity' class 2-8-0s.

The lagging for Stanier's Pacifics was, however, derived from Great Western practice, and it was a loose asbestos. It arrived in this loose state and they had been told to soak it on when the boiler was hot under test. Riddles went to the boiler testing shop late one night and found them in despair because the wet asbestos would not stick. Suddenly he remembered building stucco-finished quarters on Salisbury Plain, and the German prisoners throwing handfuls of stone and gravel at the wall surfaces with such force that the mixture stuck. He told one of the men to bring him a bucket of asbestos, and threw a handful at the boiler, to his delight it stuck. By 2.30am the boiler was beautifully and evenly covered.

On 1 July 1933, shortly after *The Princess Royal* had been successfully inspected at Euston, Riddles was trans-ferred to Euston as Stanier's assistant. He says, 'I wasn't asked to go; I was told to go.' His interview with Stanier started off with a discussion about *The Princess Royal* and future plans. This continued for some time and he wondered whether and at what point Stanier was going to come to the point of the interview. Suddenly Stanier said, 'Oh, by the way, I want you up here on Tuesday'. Riddles meekly replied, 'Yes, Sir'. As he went out of the door, Stanier added, 'The Directors agreed to double your salary'. Riddles comments, 'It was a good thing I was holding on to the door.'

Though the 12 Pacifics had been wanted badly for the heavy long distance express trains, there was a sore need to replenish the whole LMS locomotive stock. To meet immediate requirements, six new designs were prepared with a standard range of Swindon-type boilers. Stanier had decided on these because, although the parallel boilers of the 'Royal Scots' and 'Baby Scots' (officially 'Patriots', after the rebuilt LNWR 'Claughton' class war memorial engine) steamed well, their mileage between repairs was not very high. Of this Stanier boiler, R. C. Bond wrote:[2] 'Though relatively expensive in first cost, they were known to have an excellent maintenance record on the Great Western and to be capable of running large mileages between heavy repairs. The gently curved shape of their Belpaire fireboxes and generous water space round the sides of the firebox undoubtedly influenced their maintenance performance far more than the conical shape of the barrel.' It is to be noticed here that it was not the Belpaire pattern of the firebox that improved maintenance performance (for the 'Royal Scots' also had Belpaire fireboxes), but Churchward's carefully designed shape.

The very efficient boiler for which he was responsible was probably Stanier's greatest success. In a discussion on Churchward's locomotives[3] Bond said: 'It is in the work that Churchward did on the locomotive boiler that his greatest contribution is found ... It was not till Sir William Stanier introduced on the locomotives he designed, as CME of the LMS, the Swindon boiler in all its essentials that the full benefits of Churchward's work was felt. The maintenance record of all Stanier's boilers has been outstanding.' But one further step was needed to bring out the best in these boilers. Bond has written:[4] 'I think we all viewed with considerable misgivings Stanier's original adherence to low degree superheating ... on a railway which had learnt to live with the problems associated with really hot steam.' In due course the Stanier boilers were fitted with larger superheaters. The comment by Riddles on Churchward's probable reasons for adhering to low superheat has been mentioned. After Churchward's retirement there was no advance on his practice in all subsequent Great Western engines. Churchward's 2-8-0 heavy freight locomotives, for instance, worked GWR goods traffic virtually unchanged from 1903 until the end of steam.

That Stanier regarded his own 2-8-0 as merely a development of Churchward's engine is shown by a letter to me from the late R. F. Hanks, a previous Chairman of the British Transport Commission's Western Area Board. Hanks wrote to congratulate Stanier on the splendid performance of one of his 2-8-0 locomotives on the London Midland Region, when it was put on an express

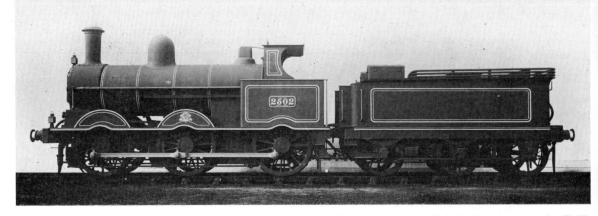

train to replace a failed diesel. 'With typical modesty,' wrote Hanks, 'Stanier replied, "Give the credit to G. J. Churchward and the Great Western".'

Whereas Stanier's two-cylinder engines were excellent from the start, there was some initial steaming trouble with the three-cylinder 'Jubilee' class 4-6-0s. Owing to a shortage of steam there were a number of failures on the Birmingham two-hour expresses, and the Operating Department, without reference to the CME's Department, transferred them to the Midland line. Riddles came back from leave as this was taking place. He immediately gave instructions that the jumper tops were to be removed at once and the diameter of the blastpipe orifice was to be reduced from $5\frac{1}{2}$in to $4\frac{7}{8}$in; for he had spotted that, far from the jumper tops being needed to reduce the blast, there was never enough of it: in fact, an arrangement that worked well with four cylinders on the GWR was not suited to the three-cylinder engines of the LMS. After the alteration had been carried out the Midland drivers declared that they had never had such fine engines.

In May 1937 the description of a big new engine was released from the CME's office. It had been designed to work fast expresses between Euston and Glasgow, and it differed from the 'Princess' class Pacifics in having increased boiler capacity, bigger cylinders, larger coupled wheels, and two sets of Walschaerts valve gear instead of four. It was intended to run at over 100mph and, to publicise its velocity, it had a streamlined casing (which both Stanier and Riddles loathed). The large coupled wheels were due to Riddles, and this he admits was a mistake. He says: 'To my shame, I suggested to Stanier that the wheel diameter might be increased to 6ft 9in. My reasons were based on a remark by J. E. Anderson that beyond a given piston speed the locomotive lost considerably in efficiency, and, as presumably only light loads were to be hauled, longer legs would be able to run faster. This I suppose is true, but I had forgotten that the engine had to start from a stand and also climb hills; and could those big wheels slip!' The size of coupled wheels was to figure in Riddles' later thinking. He never himself designed an engine with wheels bigger than 6ft 2in, and it became apparent that, with a well designed steam circuit on Châpelon principles, much smaller wheels were no bar to very fast running.

Riddles had now been Principal Assistant to the CME for four years, and had frequently acted for him in his absence. In 1834 C. E. Fairburn had been appointed Electrical Engineer to the LMS. It was now decided that he would eventually succeed Stanier and that he should accordingly be appointed Deputy CME. However, the duties envisaged for that appointment included some which were exercised by the Principal Assistant and it was therefore decided to down-grade the latter post to Locomotive Assistant. This made Riddles redundant and he was appointed Mechanical and Electrical Engineer Scotland, with an increased salary. He was not long at the former Caledonian Railway locomotive headquarters at St Rollox before he was selected to take the LMS's *Coronation Scot* train on its tour of the United States, culminating in its exhibition at the 1939 New York 'World's Fair'. The story of that tour has been related by the author in another book;[5] and it will suffice to say that, as at the start of a very lengthy journey the driver was taken ill with pneumonia, Riddles, in addition to being in charge of the train, took turns with the fireman to drive and fire No 6220 *Coronation* (actually No 6229 *Duchess of Hamilton* with exchanged number and nameplates).

Owing to the outbreak of war, Riddles again had only a brief sojourn at St Rollox, for he was loaned by the LMS to the Ministry of Supply as Director of Transportation Equipment.

Notes
Most of the information contained in this chapter was given personally to the author by Mr R. A. Riddles. Other references are given below.

1 Col H. C. B. Rogers, *The Last Steam Locomotive Engineer: R. A. Riddles, CBE* (London, George Allen & Unwin, 1970)
2 Roland C. Bond, *A Lifetime with Locomotives* (Cambridge, Goose & Son, 1975), pp103-4
3 *The Institution of Locomotive Engineers, Journal*, March-April 1950, pp182-3
4 Bond, op cit, p104
5 Rogers, op cit, p91-103

Left: A Webb 'Cauliflower' 0-6-0 express goods locomotive, displaying the LNWR badge of Britannia (after which Riddles' first Pacific for British Railways was named).
Ian Allan Library

Right: 'Sparks flying to high heaven': an 'Experiment' class 4-6-0 on the down LNWR 'Scotchman' near Bletchley.
Ian Allan Library

Below: A Churchward 'Star' class 4-6-0 No 4006 *Red Star* on the Great Western Royal train of 1897 near Chippenham on 20 July 1907. (A sister engine of No 4005 *Polar Star*.)
British Railways

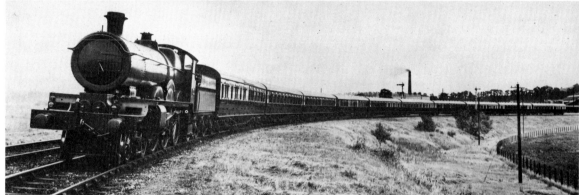

Top: No 4023 *King George*: after the advent of Collett's 'King' class 4-6-0s, the engines of the King series of 'Stars' became Monarchs, and No 4023 was renamed *Danish Monarch.* *British Railways*

Above centre: One of the last batch of Churchward's 'Stars', the Abbey series, in their original austerity livery with cast iron chimney, on 8 August 1922. It is at the head of the 'Cornish Riviera Express', composed of 'Toplight' carriages, and the first train to be painted in the re-introduced chocolate and cream livery. *British Railways*

Above: Bowen-Cooke's reply to *Polar Star*: the first of his four-cylinder 4-6-0s No 2222 *Sir Gilbert Claughton.* 'Bowen Cooke had to do something . . . A lost opportunity for the boiler was too small and inefficient'. *Ian Allan Library*

Top right: A rebuilt 'Claughton'; but: 'Even when a new and bigger boiler was fitted in later years, it never matched up to the job.' *British Railways*

Above centre right: A superheated LNWR 4-4-0, No 5000 *Coronation* of the 'George the Fifth' class — engines which performed some of the most remarkable feats for their size in the history of railways. *British Railways*

Below centre right: A superheated LNWR 4-6-0, No 819 *Prince of Wales*, the first of a class which was probably the best of all LNWR locomotive designs. *Ian Allan Library*

Right: A LNWR 0-8-0 rebuilt with a Belpaire firebox. *C. M. Kempson*

Top: LNWR 'Prince of Wales' class 4-6-0 *Robert Southey* passing South Hampstead.   *British Railways*

Above: LMS 'Royal Scot' class three-cylinder 4-6-0 No 6147 *The Northamptonshire Regiment*. *Ian Allan Library*

Top right: LMS rebuilt 'Royal Scot' class locomotive No 46169 *The Boy Scout* on the 12.5pm Manchester to Euston express.   *British Railways*

Centre right: An LMS 'Claughton' replacement 'Patriot' class (nicknamed 'Baby Scot') No 45520 *Llandudno* — one of the most successful LMS locomotive designs of its time and the precursor of Stanier's three-cylinder 'Jubilee' class 4-6-0s. *Ian Allan Library*

Right: Churchward's only Pacific, No 111 *The Great Bear* of the Great Western Railway — the precursor of Stanier's 'Princess' class on the LMS — after being fitted with top feed.   *British Railways*

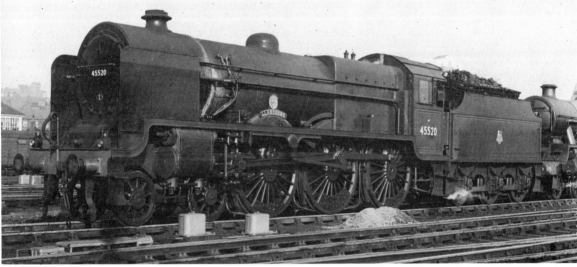

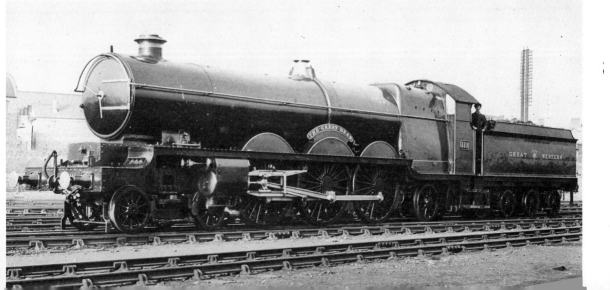

Top left: LMS 'Princess' class Pacific No 6203 Princess Margaret Rose on the 8.20am Liverpool to Euston express passing King's Langley on 20 July 1950. British Railways

Left: 'Jubilee' class engine No 45653 in the days of British Railways. The steaming troubles of this class were cured by Riddles. British Railways

Top: The up 'Coronation Scot' express hauled by the LMS streamlined Pacific locomotive with the big wheels, of which Riddles says: 'To my shame I suggested to Stanier that the wheel diameter might be increased to 6ft 9in.' British Railways

Above: No 6229 Duchess of Hamilton, temporarily designated No 6220 Coronation, hauling the eight-coach 'Coronation Scot' and embellished with an American pattern headlight, en route, for running in the USA. British Railways

Top left: The unstreamlined version: No 46244 *King George VI* on the 'Caledonian' express. *British Railways*

Left: LMS 'Duchess' class Pacific No 46227 *Duchess of Devonshire* climbing Shap. *British Railways*

Above: A Stanier Class 5 two-cylinder 4-6-0 No 45008 seen in BR days; these were the replacements for the LNWR 'Prince of Wales' class. *Ian Allan Library*

2
Engines for War

Demands on the new Directorate, of which Riddles was the head, soon came in. Locomotives were wanted, not only for the British Expeditionary Force in France, but also for North Africa and Ceylon. It had been announced in July 1938 that the War Office would need locomotives for use overseas, and as a first instalment to meet this requirement is was agreed that the Great Western Railway would supply 100 0-6-0 freight engines. Those selected were the remarkable little '2301' class of goods engines designed by William Dean in 1883, which had given outstanding service during World War 1. Their popularity was due to their simplicity, comparatively high power, and a light axle load which permitted their use on the flimsiest track. But although perhaps adequate for the immediate needs on the Lines of Communication of the small British Expeditionary Force, they were much too small for the haulage of the heavy ammunition and supply trains which, it was considered, would ultimately be required.

The idea of a standard type of steam locomotive for military purposes had led in World War 1 to the selection of the admirable 2-8-0 heavy goods engines designed in 1911 by J. G. Robinson for the Great Central Railway. Their only rivals had been G. J. Churchward's Great Western 2-8-0s; but the latter suffered from the disadvantage that, apart from the GWR with its large construction gauge, few lines in Great Britain could accommodate the greater width over their cylinders. The GC 2-8-0s were therefore chosen, though they too were built to a construction gauge that was larger than that of most of the railways which amalgamated to form the LMS, so that the large number available after the end of the war went mostly to the LNER and GWR.

The need for big freight engines being urgent, it was apparent to Riddles that he would have to make use of an existing type. Owing to the large number that still existed, he was strongly tempted to take the Robinson 2-8-0s again; but he had, with regret, to reject this idea, because over the years they had been modified in a number of ways to suit their owning companies and were no longer a standard class. New engines would therefore have to be built, but, as stated above, they would have to be of an existing type. There was really only one contender — Stanier's 2-8-0 for the LMS which was well tried and had given excellent service. Gresley's LNER 2-8-0s, with their three cylinders and conjugated valve gear, would have posed too much of a maintenance problem under active service conditions. Riddles therefore asked Stanier if he could have his help with drawings, patterns, press blocks,

etc, and also if he would agree to his Chief Draughtsman, T. F. ('Tommy') Coleman, discussing with the North British Locomotive Company the problems of production. Stanier readily agreed.

The outcome was that 240 Stanier 2-8-0s were ordered for the War Department, though only 208 of this order were actually built (158 by the North British Locomotive Company and 50 by Beyer Peacock), because the defeat of the Allied armies in France and Flanders caused the cancellation of the remaining 32. The orders were placed in December 1939 and the North British Locomotive Company delivered the first engine in May 1940, but by this time the BEF was conducting the fighting withdrawal which was to end in embarkation at Dunkirk and the neighbouring beaches. (The Author remembers seeing a Dean 0-6-0 on a stranded ammunition train.)

From May 1940 onwards, deliveries of the Stanier 2-8-0s averaged from two to two and a half per week. In addition, 51 engines which had been built for the LMS were transferred to the War Department, so that the ultimate total was 259. Locomotives were now badly needed in the Middle East and 228 were shipped to Egypt. Of these, 23 were lost at sea through enemy action. The 215 which were successfully landed were used in Persia, Palestine, Egypt and the Western Desert. Still more engines being requested, Riddles, in 1941, had after all to despatch 91 of the Robinson 2-8-0s.

By this time Riddles had been promoted to Deputy Director-General Royal Engineer Equipment, and had a greatly enlarged Directorate under his control which dealt with all engineer stores and material, and which was divided into 10 branches of which only one was concerned with locomotives and rolling stock. However we are only concerned here with this last.

The Stanier locomotives had been doing very well in the Middle East, but one difficulty had arisen. A large number of them had been fitted to burn oil fuel before being sent to Persia, where they were very satisfactory during the cooler months of the year; but the summer months of the South Persian plain, one of the hottest parts of the world, were too much for them. Andimeshk, the main British military centre at the time and an important locomotive centre, was, indeed, reputed to be the second hottest town on earth. (I must plead ignorant as to the identity of the hottest.) Whether Andimeshk's reputation is deserved or not, the Royal Air Force recorded an official shade temperature of 135 degrees Fahrenheit, and when I visited the place one day in June I was congratulated on selecting a cool day — the temperature being only 119 degrees. These sort of temperatures were too much for the LMS cold water injectors, and they refused to work. Davies and Metcalfe hot water injectors had to be sent out immediately.

Riddles' choice of Stanier's 2-8-0s resulted in their adoption, in December 1941, as the standard heavy freight engine which would be built to meet the immediate needs of all the British railway companies, so that there would be a reserve to draw on for military service if required. After completing existing orders for their own types, therefore, the principal railway works were soon turning out these LMS engines.

As the war developed, and plans for the invasion of the European continent matured, it became apparent that very many more locomotives would be needed to replace indigenous types destroyed by Allied and enemy action. In spite of the effort devoted to producing new Stanier 2-8-0s, Riddles realised that it would not be possible to build them in sufficient numbers to meet the new staff requirement. Not only did they take too long to build, but there was a serious shortage of much of the material used in them, particularly steel castings and forgings. (In each engine, for instance, there were 22tons of steel castings.) He thought again of the Robinson 2-8-0s, but again the lack of standardisation appeared to present an insuperable problem. The four British CMEs were well aware of his difficulties, and one day Sir Nigel Gresley called on him with an offer to transfer to him almost immediately all the Robinson 2-8-0s in LNER possession, if Riddles would undertake to replace them as early as possible with new engines of Gresley's 'O2' class 2-8-0 design. Riddles says: 'I was profuse in the thanks with which I rejected the offer, as I knew that I could build two, or two and a half, of the type I had in mind for every one of the 'O2' class, apart from the difficulty of finding the materials.'

Riddles now began planning an entirely new engine, which should have the minimum of attachments, be easy to prepare for running, have maximum accessibility, and be easy to maintain. The railway companies were rather disturbed by this change of policy, as was also the Ministry of Transport who had visualised the Stanier 2-8-0s being built in large numbers and bought by the railway companies at bargain prices after the war. Indeed, Sir Alan Mount, Chief Inspecting Officer of Railways, telephoned Riddles and told him that no CME of a British railway would ever consent to use the engines he proposed building. To this, Riddles retorted, 'I don't mind if you push them into the sea after we have won the war!'

The firm which was to co-operate with Riddles in the design and development of the engines (to which he had given the name of 'Austerity') was the North British Locomotive Company. A particular difficulty was that the need was so urgent that the locomotives would have to be ordered straight off the drawing board, with no possibility of testing prototypes and making subsequent alterations, because all components would have to be immediately standard, both to avoid delay in replacements and so that parts would be interchangeable between war-damaged locomotives.

The 'Austerity' 2-8-0 had some relationship to the LMS 2-8-0 because the outline scheme had been got out by F. G. Carrier, a draughtsman who was section leader in the development and design branch of the Derby drawing office.

For ease of manufacture Riddles chose a parallel boiler with round top firebox, rather than the intricate and expensive Churchward taper boiler with Belpaire firebox. The boiler had two rings, with the dome on the back one, and the front tube plate was recessed into the front ring. There was no lagging except on the firebox back plate; the air space between the boiler and its cladding being used as an insulator, as previously mentioned. The inner firebox was copper with normal brick arch and firebars. The firebox was designed so that it could be converted easily to oil burning, without taking the boiler off the frames; the only alterations necessary being to fit a false bottom to the ashpan and install oil burners at the front of the firebox. The tender, also, was designed for easy alteration to carry oil fuel.

Riddles almost eliminated steel castings, cutting down the 22ton needed for the LMS 2-8-0 to only 2½ton. Cast iron replaced steel castings for all except the centre driving wheels. The leading truck wheels were rolled in one piece, and the tender had rolled forged wheels (after an initial trial with chilled cast iron wheels had failed owing to drivers' braking habits). Balance weights were cast into the wheel centres, but reciprocating parts were left unbalanced. Steel tyres were shrunk on to the coupled wheels. Springing was compensated to give easy riding over poor tracks.

Two outside 19in by 28in cylinders drove on to the third pair of 4ft 8½in diameter coupled wheels; and piston valves, 10in in diameter, were operated by Walschaerts valve gear. Other important dimensions were a boiler pressure of 225lb/sq in, a grate area of 28.6sq ft, and an engine weight in working order of 72ton, of which 62ton were available for adhesion. Cab and footplate fittings were simplified as much as possible. With vivid memories of the trouble he had experienced with crossheads on the LMS Pacifics, Riddles chose the Laird pattern with twin bars above the piston (these having the additional advantage of being much cheaper to manufacture).

Riddles never approved of undue emphasis on thermal efficiency. The basis of his engines was a boiler that would meet all demands made of it. He says: 'Whether or not they would burn a pound or two a mile more than a more sophisticated engine, I regarded as the unrealistic preoccupation of the theorist, because in practice a good driver and fireman could save pounds if given a freesteaming engine.' This contention was to be borne out by the running of his 'Britannia' class Pacifics on the Great Eastern line 'Broadsman' express. Of the average rates of consumption per journey by the 'Britannias' with nine different crews, the lowest was 2,448gal of water and 3,060lb of coal, and the highest 3,077gal of water and 3,846lb of coal. The intermediate figures were spread fairly evenly between these.

Riddles anticipated a great deal of criticism of his 'Austerity' 2-8-0s. However, his old friend Charles Lake, Technical Editor of *The Railway Engineer*, said to him that the first thing that anybody noticed about an engine was the chimney, and added: 'If you want to avoid criticism of your designs, put a bloody funny chimney on; the critics would then concentrate on that and forget about the rest of the engine'. Riddles took that advice and put an absurdly dumpy chimney on his engine, making it 3in lower than the boiler mountings. In diverting criticism from the more controversial aspects of his design, the result was gratifying; but he was too much of an artist to countenance a really ugly chimney. (Moreover, when he came to design the later and larger 2-10-0, the chimney proved just right for the most exacting restrictions of the British loading gauge.)

Riddles awaited the appearance of his 'Austerity' 2-8-0s with some natural anxiety, and on 23 November 1942 he wrote to W. Lorimer, Chairman of the North British Locomotive Company, asking him to do all in his power to get the first engine out by the end of the year at the latest. He added: 'I think you are aware of the antagonism of the Chief Mechanical Engineers to this engine, and our one hope of getting it running on the British railways is to produce it at a time when they are desperately in need of power and will be forced to take it in hand. When this has been done, I am quite sure that the locomotive itself will prove so effective in service that all criticisms will be overridden and it should be accepted with joy by the operators.'

Lorimer replied on 25 November regretting that there appeared to be no possibility of steaming the first 'Austerity' engine that year owing to difficulties over supplies, material, labour, and existing contracts. However, he failed only by a fortnight to meet Riddles' date for the first engine, which was handed over on 16 January 1943. It had been built in five months from the date of placing the order, and after all the parts had been delivered it was assembled in 10 days — a record, incidentally, for the North British Locomotive Company. When it was sent to St Rollox shed for trial, the driver, William McPherson, was interviewed by the *Glasgow Herald*, and said: 'This is the first time I have had a cushioned seat for my work, and altogether I have never handled a better engine.'

Production was rapid, because, owing to the simplicity of the design and the use of more readily available materials, thousands of man-hours were saved and time lost in waiting for parts was drastically cut. Whereas the LMS 2-8-0s were being built at a rate of from two to two-and-a-half a week, the rate for the 'Austerities' was, from the start, between five and six a week, and with the help of other manufacturers this soon rose to seven per week.

Although the risk had been taken of building the engines directly off the drawing board, Riddles' visits to Glasgow every week end and his careful supervision of every aspect of design and construction resulted in the engines having no teething troubles, other than the quickly remedied ones of the tender wheels and a weakness in the control springs between engine and tender. But it was an anxious time for him because these locomotives, built without prototype or trial, eventually numbered 935 — the largest class of British locomotives ever built, except for the 943 'DX' class 0-6-0 goods engines built by Ramsbottom for the London & North Western and Lancashire & Yorkshire Railways between

1858 and 1874. But Ramsbottom had many years to modify his engines if necessary, whereas Riddles had none, and he says that the decision to order such a large number before a single one had been built required courage, because there were so many critics of his policy 'who were only awaiting a chance to pounce'. Of the 935, the North British Locomotive Company built 545 and the Vulcan Foundry 390.

The 'Austerity' 2-8-0s were turned out in advance of military needs, and 450 were lent to the British railway companies: 350 going to the LNER, 50 to the LMS, and 50 to the Southern. The GWR, which originally had none, acquired 72 from the LNER, eight from the LMS, and nine from the Southern. They were an immediate success, even on the somewhat parochial Great Western. The LNER got their first engine in February 1943, and it made its first run hauling a goods train over the West Highland line. In his book, *Steam Locomotives*, Mr O. S. Nock quotes a very senior officer at York, who loved North Eastern engines, as saying that the 'WDs' were by far the best freight engines they had ever had. They were found to be powerful and quick starters, moving away rapidly with anything up to 80 wagons, and comparing well with the American 2-8-0s, built for the operations in Europe, which were rather laboured starters. LNER men, indeed, said that the 'Austerities' were better than the LMS type 2-8-0s which were working on that railway, and there was a considerable body of opinion that considered them faster than the popular Robinson 2-8-0s.

The War Office were so pleased with Riddles' engines that they asked him for a similar type of locomotive with the same tractive effort, but with 13½ton axle load instead of the 2-8-0s' 15½ton. The reason for this request was that long and heavy trains would probably have to be hauled over light, improvised, or imperfect track, on which an engine axle load of 13½ton was about the maximum. This presented a problem. Riddles first thought of a 2-8-2, but felt that this would sacrifice adhesion (*Edith Cavell* again!), and decided that a 2-10-0 was the right answer. With the extra pair of coupled wheels it could have a bigger boiler without exceeding the stipulated axle load, and a wide firebox would be a help with indifferent fuel. To enable it to run through a 4½ chain curve, he decided that the centre coupled wheels should be flangeless and that those on either side of them should have flanges of reduced thickness. This decision caused some anxiety at the North British Locomotive Company, but Riddles insisted. He had curves laid out and calculated that with a wider wheel tread all would be well. The first of the new engines to be completed was taken to St Rollox shed, and was just about to go through a sharp curve, when a ganger, who happened to be there, ran up waving his arms and protesting that the curve was far too sharp to take an engine of that length. To his astonishment, it went through the curve without even the usual 'grind' of a 2-8-0. Riddles says that they got, in effect, the equivalent of an articulated engine, because, with the flangeless wheels and possible slight flexing of the frames, the 2-10-0 was very easy on curves.

After the war, when the LMS was asked to take over some of these 2-10-0s, the Civil Engineers objected to using them until they could test the 'throw-over' on a 1 in 8 curve at a station platform. The argument about this went on for some time, and Riddles believes that there was difficulty in finding such a condition. He got tired of waiting and telephoned General McMullen, asking if he would make a test at Longmoor, where he knew there was a 1 in 8 crossing at the station. This was on a Saturday morning, but by the Monday he had received a highly satisfactory chart of the complete test. He presented this to the Chief Engineer, who then agreed to the engines being used.

As regards the details of the 'Austerity' 2-10-0s, much of it was common with the 2-8-0s, including the dimensions of the cylinders. The 2-10-0 boiler, however, besides being larger and longer, incorporated a wide steel firebox with 40sq ft grate area and three arch tubes — the latter being a very unusual feature for a British locomotive. In addition, the firebox extended into the barrel to form a combustion chamber. Riddles decided on a more orthodox lagging of the boiler, with asbestos mattress, because of the extremes of temperature to which it might be subjected in the Middle East theatres of war. All the 2-10-0s, 150 of them, were manufactured by the North British Locomotive Company.

The first of Riddles' 2-10-0s was turned out by the North British Locomotive Company in June 1944. It was unquestionably one of the masterpieces of British locomotive design, and it was the progenitor of the '9F' class 2-10-0s that he designed for British Railways. The first 20 engines were despatched to the Middle East, and they were in fact the earliest of the 'Austerity' locomotives to be sent overseas. Sixteen of them were initially put into store in Egypt, while the remaining four went into service on the Damas Hama & Prolongments Railways in Syria and the Lebanon.

Some interesting comments on these four engines (with preliminary mention of the '9Fs') are contained in two letters to the author from Col K. R. M Cameron. In the first letter he writes as follows: 'The story of the "90 with a 9F" is well known, and I remember being surprised in Paddington one day to see the "Red Dragon" express leave behind a "9F". I only once travelled on the footplate of this class and can understand why they could be employed on express passenger services: they steam exceptionally well, and the riding was very smooth, probably because of the lengthy rigid wheelbase. This was a characteristic of the wartime class: we had four of these working, on loan, on the Syrian Railways, and I can remember the first passenger train working when one worked the "Taurus Express" from Aleppo to the Turkish frontier at Medaine Ekbes. Express is hardly the word to use for this relatively slow train, although in accordance with the traditional French practice the engine had to be fitted with a Flaman speed recorder before it was allowed to work a passenger train! However, its smoothness on the rather indifferent track and severe curves impressed me, as the driver. On the sharp curves of the Haifa-Beirut Railway the GC ROD 2-8-0 engines had to have their tyres reprofiled every 5,000 miles or so, but the 2-10-0 rode these curves like a Pullman car. No doubt that characteristic passed on to the postwar "9Fs".'

With his second letter Cameron enclosed several photographs. The first shows 2-10-0 No 3688 at Aleppo on the northbound 'Taurus Express' with Cameron himself as the driver (then Lt-Col, Royal Engineers, commanding No 2 Railway Workshop Group). He says: 'You will note that the whistle has departed from its usual horizontal position: this was done because all trains on the DHP had no continuous brakes but depended on caboose brakemen who applied or released handbrakes from their cabooses in answer to whistle signals from the locomotive. On the Syrian plain, where winds often reached gale force, the brakemen complained that with the horiontal whistle they could not hear the whistle signals, with the result that some train journeys became decidedly hazardous on some of the steeper falling gradients!' Another photograph shows the same engine at Medain Ekbes after having detached from the 'Taurus Express'. Of the remaining two photographs, Cameron says that they 'show the TCDD. (Turkish State Railways) 2-10-0 No 56.087 which took over the train for the journey to Ankara and Istanbul. These were Henschel built and were truly enormous machines. We had two of these from Adana to Ulukisla, 44 miles at 1 in 40!! The combined tractive effort was 104,000lb, and on the crawl up the Taurus gorge at full throttle, with all their electric lights on, and two fountains of fire from the chimneys, the sight in the darkness was stupendous.'

Regarding the performance of the 2-8-0s and 2-10-0s in France and Flanders, Maj-Gen D. J. McMullen, Director of Transportation, wrote to Riddles on 15 February 1945 as follows:

'My dear Riddles, I am just back from a short visit to BLA (British Liberation Army) and felt I must write and tell you how excellently the Austerities & 2-10-0s are performing. Everyone loves the 2-10-0. It is quite the best freight engine ever turned out in Great Britain and does well on even Belgian "duff" which is more like porridge than coal. The 2-8-0s have trouble for steam on this muck alone, but if they can get 25% of Dutch lump coal mixed with it they do all right.

'It is amazing to trundle along at 60 kilometers per hour on a 2-8-0 Austerity in full daylight only three miles from the Bosch front line! In Nijmegen station, standing on the footplate one could see the shell bursts in the battle area so your products are well up into the fighting area, often *ahead* of the medium artillery positions.

'I am off to India on Tuesday for four weeks.'

Of McMullen, Riddles wrote to the author recently: 'He was a dedicated steam man and loved to drive engines ... On one occasion he told me that 95% of his equipment was successfully landed for the Egypt campaign. Since we had designed some of it and delivered most of it, we were more than pleased.'

These very competent engines were in great demand by various administrations after the war was over. Most of those in Europe returned to the United Kingdom and were soon in widespread use by the railway companies. After nationalisation the British Transport Commission purchased 533 2-8-0s and 25 2-10-0s. The Crown Agents bought 12 of the 2-8-0s and sent them to Hong Kong, where they worked both passenger and freight trains over the 23 miles to the Chinese border.

Of those remaining in Europe, 184 2-8-0s and 103 2-10-0s were purchased by the Dutch Government and were extensively used on all classes of trains until electrification of the main lines was completed in 1949. Thereafter, they were used for some years more on freight trains, and after their final withdrawal, two of the 2-8-0s were bought by the Swedish Railways.

The 16 2-10-0s in Egypt were sold to the Hellenic Railways in Greece, which had an urgent need for locomotives after the ravages of war. They were used on all types of traffic from international expresses to local goods trains. All were still in service in the late 1970s. Finally, the four 2-10-0s in Syria were still working trains there in 1972.

Few classes of steam locomotives can have acquired such far-flung popularity.

Riddles had returned to the LMS by the time the first of the 'Austerity' 2-10-0s was completed. Stanier, who was still CME, walked into Riddles' office one Saturday saying, 'Bad luck, Robert'. Riddles had at that moment been told by one of his former staff at the Ministry of Supply that seven or eight of the 2-10-0s had been stopped at Peterborough with broken stays in the firebox. He asked Stanier how he knew as he had only just got the information himself. Stanier replied that it had been given out over the 'tin can'. (This was the name given to the daily telephone conference, held under the authority of the then Railway Executive, between operating officers of all railways and at which were reported and discussed arrangements for traffic control, untoward incidences, etc.) Riddles was naturally very worried and, being Saturday, he returned early to his home at Watford, from whence he set off by car for Peterborough. Just as he arrived at Peterborough station to enquire the whereabouts of the running shed, he saw, coming round the corner, Tom Lawson, the North British Works Super-

intendent. Seeing Riddles, his face broke into a broad grin, and he said 'The bloody fools have been tapping the flexible stays!' (Normally when stays are tapped with a hammer they give a ring if they are sound and a dull thud if they are not; but flexible stays, being linked together, also respond to a tap with a dull thud.) Riddles says: 'I breathed a sigh of relief, and how we both enjoyed it!'

The high regard that the North British Locomotive Company had for Riddles was marked by the firm's presentation to him of a golden key to their Hydepark Works.

Riddles experienced considerable strains and frustrations during his time at the Ministry of Supply, and at one time interference by other Directorates impelled him to seek an interview with the Second Secretary concerned. This Second Secretary (later Permanent Under-Secretary at the War Office) was a very remarkable man. He told the Author that behind his desk at the Ministry of Supply there hung a picture frame into which it was his practice to insert a picture calculated to influence a visitor the way he desired. When Riddles came to see him on this occasion the frame held a very large photograph of an 'Austerity' engine. 'When this caught Riddles' eye,' said Sir George, 'there came into his face the sort of fatuous expression with which a very young man regards the female object of his affection.' The purpose of the visit was forgotten, and Riddles was diverted into discussing the features and performance of his engine!

For his services with the Ministry of Supply, Riddles was honoured by being appointed a CBE.

Notes

Except where otherwise stated, I am indepted to Mr R. A. Riddles for most of the information contained in this chapter.

For some of the detail I have found the following book of value: *Heavy Goods Engines of the War Department, Vol 3, Austerity 2-8-0 and 2-10-0*, by J. W. P. Rowledge (Poole, Springhead Books, 1978)

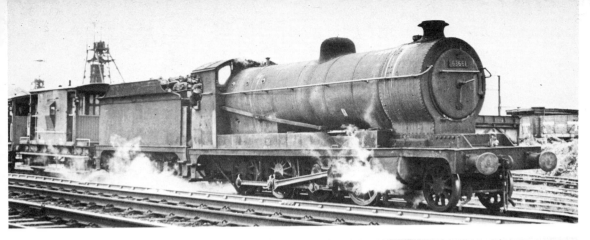

Far left: Great Western '2301' class 0-6-0 No 2513 — outstanding military service in two world wars.
Ian Allan Library

Top: Robinson Great Central Railway 2-8-0 as British Railways No 63661. The most notable army locomotive of World War 1 and fine performer in the Middle East during World War 2.
G. H. Marsh

Above: GWR '28xx' class 2-8-0 on a freight train passing High Wycombe. An admirable type but too wide over the cylinders for general wartime use.
British Railways

Left: Stanier's 8F 2-8-0 No 48400; one of a class originally built for the LMS. Excellent engines and the only ones at the start of World War 2 that met the military requirements. *J. B. Bucknall*

Above: Gresley's LNER 2-8-0 No 3833; one of a fine class, but the three cylinders and conjugated valve gear would have presented too great a maintenance problem for general military service. *British Railways*

Left: One of Riddles' 'Austerity' 2-8-0s under the coaling tower at Thornton MPD in Scotland, with its 'bloody funny' chimney. *G. P. Cooper*

Above right: 'Austerity' 2-8-0 No 90662 on an up coal train near Watford. *British Railways*

Right: 'Austerity' 2-8-0 No 90558 at Toton on 22 May 1965. *G. L. Allen*

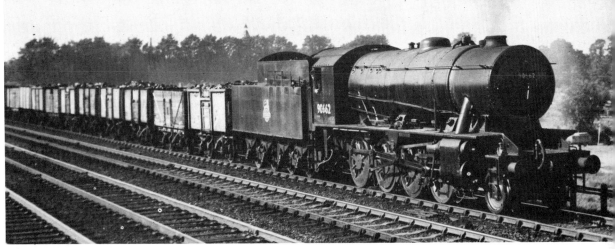

Left: 'Austerity' 2-8-0 No 90045 and Class J27 (NER 'P3' class) 0-6-0 inside a roundhouse at York MPD on 4 October 1964. *Brian Stephenson*

Above: 'Austerity' 2-10-0 No 3688 at the Turkish frontier station of Mekdaine Ekbes, after being detached from the 'Taurus Express'. *Col K. R. M. Cameron*

Below left: Riddles 'Austerity' 2-10-0 No 3688 at Aleppo on the northbound 'Taurus Express' on 20 August 1944, driven by Lt-Col K. R. M. Cameron, Royal Engineers, commanding No 2 Railway Workshop Group. *Col K. R. M. Cameron*

Below: Turkish State Railways 2-10-0 No 56.087 backing on to the 'Taurus Express' at Mekdaine Ekbes in replacement of the Riddles engine. *Col K. R. M. Cameron*

3
The Railway Executive

Riddles returned to the LMS on 1 August 1943 as Chief Stores Superintendent. In January 1946 he was promoted to Vice-President of the LMS for Engineering. It was the appointment which, above all, he would have liked best, for to him there reported the Chief Mechanical Engineer, the Chief Civil Engineer, the Chief Signal Engineer, and the Chief Stores Superintendent. The CME was Riddles' friend H. G. Ivatt, so that their positions were now reversed as compared with the days when Riddles had been Ivatt's assistant at Derby. However, the shadow of nationalisation was already hanging over the four big railway companies, and there was considerable sadness on the LMS at the approaching end of a great company — a company which many felt was the most efficient and forward-looking in Great Britain.

Before the end of 1947 the Ministry of Transport, with vivid recollections of his wartime services, sent for Riddles and offered him the post of Member for Mechanical and Electrical Engineering on the new Railway Executive. The appointment was roughly equivalent to that of Chief Mechanical Engineer on one of the old companies, but with considerably greater powers.

On 1 January 1948 the four mainline railway companies and London Transport were nationalised and placed under the British Transport Commission, of which Sir Cyril (later Lord) Hurcomb was Chairman. The various activities controlled by the Transport Commission were managed by five public authorities called Executives. Of these, the Railway Executive consisted of five full time members and two who were part time. The Chairman of the Executive was Sir Eustace Missenden, late General Manager of the Southern Railway. It was responsible for the railways previously under the ownership of the four big companies. The members corresponded, in general to the chief officers of the old companies.

Riddles faced a formidable task, having to deal with the four eminent Chief Mechanical Engineers of the former companies, each of whom firmly believed in his own policies; and to evolve from these policies one that would be suitable for the whole of British Railways would entail considerable tact and inevitably possible disagreement. The selection of his own staff was of obvious inportance and, in spite of the need to appear neutral as between the former companies, he felt he must take men whose abilities he knew, and that meant that the majority would have to come from the LMS. He chose R. C. Bond to be responsible for locomotive construction and maintenance. Bond had lately been Mechanical Engineer (Locomotive

Works), responsible to the CME for supervising and co-ordinating the activities of all the Locomotive Works on the LMS. E. Pugson also came from the LMS to look after carriage and wagon construction and maintenance. On the LMS he had been Bond's opposite number at Derby as Chief Officer Carriage and Wagon Construction and Maintenance. Riddles' Electrical Engineer was C. M. Cock from the Southern (later to be relieved by S. B. Warder for the same company). Cock had been Chief Electrical Engineer. The Superintendent of Motive Power was another LMS man, H. Rudgard, who had held the same position on his old Company. He was responsible jointly to Riddles and to the Operating Member, V. M. Barrington-Ward (late Assistant General Manager, Operating LNER).

It was apparent to Riddles that the main weakness in his organisation was that, unlike a normal CME, he had no chief draughtsman. Chief draughtsmen were senior officers of long and varied experience who translated their CME's intentions into the finished article, or even designed an engine to meet a very generally worded CME specification. (Responsibility for a locomotive, falls squarely on the shoulders of a CME; and those, other than he, who sometimes claim the credit for success, are noticeably less ready to accept the blame for failure.) It was obvious to Riddles that he must have a chief draughtsman. It was equally obvious that he could not deal with each of the chief draughtsmen of the old companies, nor could he select any one of them because the result would inevitably favour the design practice of the company concerned. He got over the difficulty by the ingenious idea of establishing a kind of corporate chief draughtsman. He formed the Chief Draughtsmen of Derby, Doncaster, Swindon and Brighton into a committee under the chairmanship of E. S. Cox from the LMS as Executive Officer Design.

The reasons which underlay Riddles' choice of steam as the motive power for British Railways and his decision to embark on a new range of designs have been discussed elsewhere.[1] It will suffice to say here that at the prices current in 1950 steam locomotives were by far the cheapest in both capital cost and cost per drawbar horsepower, and that the circumstances of the time demanded engines which, though incorporating all that was best in modern practice, should be simple to drive, easy to maintain, and able to run with indifferent fuel.

Having decided on steam, studies led to the conclusion that 12 different types of locomotives would meet all requirements. We are concerned with only one of these 12 types, the heavy freight engine; but before discussing it, it is necessary to outline those features which were common to all or some of the Riddles family of engines.

Firstly, in view of postwar shortages of technical manpower and the difficult maintenance conditions, he insisted that everything should be 'get-at-able'. From this it naturally followed that wherever possible there should be two cylinders only and that they should be outside. Their valve gear, too, should obviously be outside, and, pending any future decision to adopt valve gear, the well-tried Walshaerts arrangement was an understandable selection.

The larger locomotives were to have wide fireboxes. The advantage of these had been demonstrated by the 'Austerity' 2-10-0s, in their ability to cope with poor fuel, and by the steam-raising capacity of all the British Pacifics (following, of course, the lead of the Great Northern Atlantics). Less obviously, the Belpaire type of firebox was adopted. A reason given for this choice was to assure ample volume for the disengagement of steam in the area of maximum evaporation.[2] It would be difficult, however, to justify this contention. LNER Pacifics and 'B1' 4-6-0s certainly never suffered in this respect in comparison with their LMS opposite numbers; and Riddles incorporated round-top fireboxes on his very successful 'Austerities'. He says, in fact, that there is little to choose between either type, except that there is perhaps some advantage in staying the two flat surfaces of the Belpaire inner and outer fireboxes, as compared with staying a flat-top inner firebox to a round-top outer one. The merits of the Churchward firebox lay rather in the careful design of its sweeping curves rather than the Belpaire top. Churchward himself, in his famous paper of 1906 *Large Locomotive Boilers*, said: 'The flat top has the important advantage of increasing the area of the water-line at the hottest part of the boiler and so materially contributes to the reduction of foaming.' But Churchward's engines did not have a dome. The late André Chapelon pointed out, in a letter to the Author, that Patrick Stirling, with the domeless boilers of his engines, avoided the risk of priming by lowering the top of the inner firebox, but that such a reduction was not acceptable in Great Western engines because they had to work so much harder. He added that Churchward, to avoid reducing the circulation, increased the distance between the tops of the inner and outer firebox by raising and flattening the latter. Bulleid, coming from the LNER, did, it is true, use Belpaire fireboxes on his Pacifics, but he had never liked the round-top firebox because the boiler fitted to the first Great Northern 'K2' class 2-6-0 developed a slight bulging during the pressure test. The reason that Riddles chose the Churchward type Belpaire firebox, as developed on the LMS, was because of its proved excellence and low cost of maintenance.

The firebox was of copper, rather than steel, because it was considered that the indifferent quality of the water available over a large part of British Railways might cause corrosion and cracking of steel fireboxes.

All locomotives were to have rocking grates, self-cleaning smokeboxes, and self-emptying ash pans.

Particular attention was paid to the steam circuit in the light of Chapelon's remarkable demonstrations. In his famous rebuilding of the Paris-Orleans Pacifics, he doubled the cross-sectional area of the steam passages, eliminated sharp bends in the steam pipes, and increased the volume of the steam chests. (It is curious that the first to appreciate the importance of large steam passages was that eminent British locomotive engineer Thomas Russell Crampton, whose first two engines were built in 1846. In Great Britain, however, no locomotive engineer seems to have noticed the easy steam flow that did so much to make the Crampton engines the success they were in France and Germany). All the Riddles engines had large straight ports and passagers for the cylinders, and the larger engines had 11in diameter piston valves. The maximum valve travel was $7\frac{1}{4}$in, which was more than that of any previous class of British locomotives; furthermore, the travel was over 4in at 20% cut-off which would have been accepted as a maximum value in earlier practice.

Draughting had been the subject of tests carried out at Rugby and Swindon, and the pattern adopted was based on these tests. It had been shown that double and other special blast pipe arrangements could give improved results at maximum output, but were inferior in performance at lesser outputs. Through the whole range of working they were less satisfactory than the single blastpipe. Because the majority of locomotive work demands less than the maximum output, the single blastpipe and chimney were retained on most of the engines. In addition, work carried out by S. O. Ell at Swindon showed the importance of having single chimneys correctly proportioned. He had found, for instance, that a reduction in the diameter of the chimney of an Ivatt LMS Class 4 2-6-0 at its narrowest point by $1\frac{1}{2}$in, together with a redution in the taper, almost doubled the steam production. The Ell type chimney was, however, somewhat narrow, and to improve the appearance of the locomotives the various chimneys were made as double-walled castings; the inner wall conforming to the required dimensions.

A number of engines were indeed fitted with double chimneys, including 80 of the '9F' class. Locomotives so equipped were those likely to be employed on duties demanding a greater margin of performance. As an example, Class 4 4-6-0s, which had to work trains normally within the province of Class 5 4-6-0s, over routes for which the axle weights of the latter were too high, were given double chimneys. The '9F' 2-10-0s, were so extensively in demand for very heavy duties, that the 80 engines with double chimneys included 67 of the last 68 to be built. The late R. C. Bond told the Author that the double chimneys on these engines proved their worth; but that the 'Britannia' class Pacifics did not have to work hard often enough to justify their provision.

At the request of Cox, formerly of the Lancashire & Yorkshire Railway, Riddles agreed to adopt the shape of that company's chimneys for his Standard engines. However, he gave instructions that the Class 9F 2-10-0s were to have the chimney which he designed for his 'Austerity' engines, to demonstrate the continuity with his earlier 2-10-0s. Unfortunately, by the time the first of the

'9Fs' came into service, Riddles had resigned from British Railways and it was adorned with the LYR pattern chimney. In retrospect, it seems a pity that the 'Austerity' chimney was not put on all the steam locomotives built for British Railways, which would then have displayed a distinctive Riddles 'signature'. As to why Riddles' instruction was not carried out is something of a mystery. F. G. Carrier, who was section leader in the development and design branch of the Derby drawing office, made an arrangement drawing of the locomotive which is no longer in existence, but the diagram by K. W. Everett, which accompanied it, shows the 'Austerity' chimney. (Carrier was, indeed, largely responsible for what both Stanier's and Riddles' engines looked like.) Riddles had also given instructions that there was to be a family resemblance between all his engines; a resemblance which should differ as far as possible from the locomotives of any one Region. It will have been noticed that the rebuilt Bulleid Pacifics were brought so ingeniously into the 'family' that they bore a close resemblance to the 'Britannias'. Nevertheless, the engines had of necessity a somewhat LMS look about them because some were merely modifications of LMS types, which had to be incorporated into the 'family' appearance.

It had been decided to fit the larger engines with roller bearings on all the coupled wheels, but Riddles was not quite convinced that these very expensive components were really necessary. He accordingly had five 'Britannias' built with roller bearings on the driving wheels only, whilst the other coupled wheels had plain bearings of LMS design. The results were so satisfactory that he had 10 more 'Britannia' Pacifics turned out with plain bearings on all the coupled wheels. Comparison in service showed no advantage to those with roller bearings. Riddles decided, therefore, that the Class 9F 2-10-0s should have plain bearings on all the coupled wheels. Subsequently these engines were to run at 90mph without any sign of distress in their axle boxes.

To arrive at the best design for the locomotive cab, Riddles had a full scale mock-up of the cab (with boiler fittings and controls in the proposed positions) built at Derby, in order that those who would drive and fire the new engines should have a chance to express their opinions on the proposed layout. The mock-up was brought to Marylebone and installed in the headquarters of the Railway Executive on 5 December 1949. There it was inspected, discussed and criticised by motive power superintendents, running shed foremen, drivers and union representatives. It was Riddles' intention that the drivers should be able to operate a locomotive from the sitting position; and the regulator, brake, and all the other controls operated by the driver were so placed that he could do this. The reversing wheel was normally positioned broadside on to the driver, but Riddles, with, as he put it, his domestic mind, had it placed end on, on the grounds that no woman could have managed a mangle with its broadside to her face. The feature which surprised and pleased some of the Great Western drivers was that they would be able to drive sitting down, which they had never been able to do on their own engines.

Having dealt with the principal features common to all or some of the Riddles 'Standard' engines, it is now time to turn to the type with which we are chiefly concerned — the heavy freight locomotive.

Because of the very large numbers of 'Austerity' and LMS 2-8-0s transferred to the railways in the United Kingdom after the war, there were plenty of heavy freight locomotives available to the Railway Executive in 1948; but it was foreseen that there would be a need before long for new and more powerful engines. The main reason for this was the likelihood that all freight rolling stock would soon be fitted with continuous brakes. The major obstacle in the past to this measure had been the large number of privately owned wagons, the owners of which were opposed to undertaking such an expensive conversion; but virtually all the private wagons had by now been incorporated into British Railways stock. It is true that the existing 2-8-0 locomotives had ample tractive effort to haul trains of the maximum length that could fit into the existing refuge sidings, so that the working of longer freight trains was not envisaged. But continuous brakes would permit such freight trains to be hauled at far higher speeds. The 2-8-0s had been designed specifically to haul trains at the low maximum speeds which the limited brake power permitted. Future developments in freight traffic would inevitably move towards the higher speeds possible in safety with continuous brakes than towards heavier loads. To meet this requirement more horsepower at speed would be necessary rather than higher tractive effort.

A proposal for a 2-8-2 with the same boiler as the 'Britannia' class 4-6-2 and with 5ft 3in coupled wheels was prepared by Cox and his committee of Chief Draughtsman, and Bond too regarded this as the obvious answer.[3] He believed that eight-coupled wheels would provide adequate adhesion weight, that the coupled wheels should be rather larger than the 4ft 8in, or thereabouts then common, and that a much larger boiler than those carried by the contemporary 2-8-0s was an essential requisite. A memorandum setting out 10 good reasons why a 2-10-0 would not be suitable was prepared in support of the argument for a 2-8-2.[4] This was obviously aimed at Riddles, whose preference for a 10-coupled freight engine was well known. The basis of the argument was the restriction imposed by the loading gauge. Firstly, a wide firebox would be essential to provide sufficient grate area, and this would of necessity be disposed, in a 2-10-0, above the rear pair of coupled wheels. This would, it was held, so limit the diameter of the boiler barrel, and thus the firebox volume and free area through the tubes, that maximum steam production would be heavily restricted. Secondly, it was believed that the minimum vertical space needed for the wide firebox above the coupled wheels would limit them to a greatest diameter of 4ft 10in.

The argument, however, was built up on a fallacy. A steam locomotive in starting, or when working slowly up a heavy gradient, tends to 'sit back' on its trailing wheels; thus transferring some of its adhesive weight to the rear. If the trailing wheels are uncoupled, therefore, there will under these conditions be a loss of adhesion. It is well known, for instance, that Pacific locomotives are more prone to slip on starting than the sure-footed 4-6-0s. A 2-8-2 when starting, therefore, would have actually *less* adhesion than a 2-8-0. There was no prospect, indeed, that Riddles, having rejected a 2-8-2 wheel arrangement for this very reason when designing his larger 'Austerity' engine, would accept it as suitable for the haulage of fast heavy freight trains on British Railways. He did not, furthermore, agree that driving wheels as large as 5ft 3in were necessary for fast speeds with an engine having a well-designed steam circuit, and he believed that there was sufficient space within the loading gauge for a boiler of adequate size. He said that he wanted a 2-10-0 and requested Cox and his committee to think again and see if 5ft diameter coupled wheels could be accommodated under a wide firebox. That this was indeed possible was in due course confirmed. That he was correct in his views was demonstrated, of course, by the outstanding performance of the resultant 2-10-0s in traffic. The coupled wheelbase was given the same form of flexibility which Riddles had designed for the 'Austerity' 2-10-0s. It had been intended to have the 'Britannia' boiler, but this was not practicable within the loading gauge because of the necessity to pitch it high enough to clear the trailing coupled wheels. The maximum diameter at the back end

was therefore 6ft 1in, as compared with the 6ft 5½in of the 'Britannia'; though both had the same diameter of 5ft 9in at the front end. The length between tube plates was 15ft 3in for the 2-10-0 and 17ft for the 'Britannia', and the 2-10-0 had a grate area of 40.2sq ft whilst the 'Britannia's' was slightly larger at 42sq ft. Cylinder dimensions of 20in by 28in were the same for both engines. The axle weights of the 2-10-0 were only 15ton 10cwt, which was less than that of any other of the British Railways 'Standard' engines except the Class 2 2-6-0 and Class 2 2-6-2 tank engine. Detail design of the Class 9F 2-10-0 was allocated to Brighton.

Notes

Except where otherwise stated, I am indebted again to Mr R. A Riddles for most of the information contained in this chapter.

1 Col H. C. B. Rogers, *Transition from Steam* (London, Ian Allan, 1980) pp6-8
2 E. S. Cox, *Standard Steam Locomotives* (London, Ian Allan, 1966), p77
3 Roland C. Bond, *A Lifetime with Locomotives* (Cambridge, Goose & Son, 1975), pp208-10
4 ibid

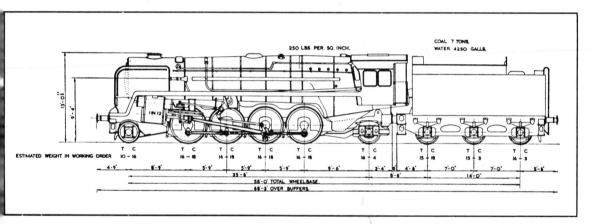

Above: The proposed 2-8-2 locomotive.

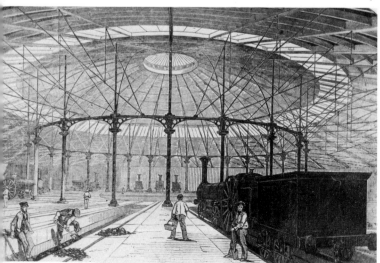

Left: A Crampton locomotive in Robert Stephenson's Roundhouse at Chalk Farm LNWR, which was built in 1847 and shown new in this illustration.
Ian Allan Library

Left: A Lancashire & Yorkshire Railway Atlantic locomotive No 1403, showing the pattern of chimney adopted by Aspinall for that railway. *Ian Allan Library*

Below left: A Riddles 'Clan' class locomotive No 72002 *Clan Campbell* near Tebay on a Glasgow-Manchester express, showing the lines adopted to provide the 'family resemblance' of the British Railway locomotives and the LYR pattern chimney. *British Railways*

Bottom left: LNER 'P1' class 2-8-2 heavy freight locomotive No 2393. *Modern Transport*

Right: '9F' class 2-10-0 No 92133 leaving Eastleigh on a 'Bromford' oil train. *R. Puntis*

Below: A 'Bromford' on the Lickey incline headed by a '9F' class 2-10-0 No 92248 with a banker at the rear. *Derek Cross*

Above left: A mixed freight train, including unfitted Esso tanker wagons ascending the Lickey incline with two '9F' 2-10-0s — No 92007 at the head and No 92079 at the rear — on 5 June 1962. *Anthony A. Vickers*

Below left: '9F' 2-10-0 No 92135 at the head of Esso tanker wagons near Bristol on the Western Region. *Ian Allan Library*

Above right: '9F' 2-10-0 No 92204 passing through Radstock on trial over the S&D line on 29 March 1960. *Ivo Peters*

Right: No 92204's trial: taking water at Evercreech Junction on the return run over the S&D on 29 March 1960. *Ivo Peters*

Below: '9F' No 92206 on a Bristol to Bournemouth train at Shepton Mallet on the S&D line June 1960. *Derek Cross*

Top left: On the Somerset & Dorset line, double chimney '9F' 2-10-0 No 92204 on a Bournemouth to Bradford train in the Masbury Summit cutting on 20 August 1960. *Ivo Peters*

Centre left: '9F' No 92203 on the 7.35am (Saturdays only) train from Nottingham to Bournemouth, sweeping through the curves south of Wellow on the S&D line on 23 July 1960. *Ivo Peters*

Left: '9F' No 92212 emerging from the Winsor Hill Tunnel on a Bristol to Bournemouth tour on 26 August 1961. *G. W. Morrison*

Top: '9F' No 92210 near Shepton Montague, S&D line, with the Saturday's only 7.40am train from Bradford to Bournemouth on 21 July 1962. *Ivo Peters*

Above: '9F' No 92233 at Templecombe (Lower) on the Somerset & Dorset line with the down 'Pines Express' on 28 June 1962. This is the engine which recorded the astounding performance narrated by R. Nelson. *Derek Cross*

Above left: No 92220 *Evening Star* on the 3.40pm Bournemouth to Bath train leaving Wincanton on the S&D line, 18 August 1962. *G. A. Richardson*

Left: The last up 'Pines Express' leaving Blandford Forum on 8 September 1962 behind 2-10-0 No 92220 *Evening Star*. *G. A. Richardson*

Above: No 92220 *Evening Star* on the last down 'Pines Express', passing Midsomer Norton, S&D line, on the steep 1 in 50 climb to Masbury. *Ivo Peters*

Centre right: No 92002 on a Poole to Newcastle express at Basingstoke (note the conductor rails). *A. Swain*

Below right: No 92220 *Evening Star* at Salisbury in August 1956 on a Portsmouth to Cardiff train. At the other platform is a LSWR Urie 'S15' class 4-6-0 No 504, a sister engine of which is being restored by the Urie S15 Preservation Group on the Mid-Hants Railway. *G. R. Wheeler*

Above: '9F' 2-10-0 No 92209 bringing a railway society special train into Bournemouth Central. On the right is 'Britannia' class Pacific No 70020 *Mercury* which worked the special from Waterloo to Salisbury and which is waiting to haul it back to Waterloo. *A. Richardson*

Below: No 92220 *Evening Star* approaching Stewarts Lane, shortly after leaving Victoria on a 'Farewell to Steam' rail tour to Yeovil Junction on 20 September 1964. *Brian Stephenson*

Right: No 92203 climbing the bank from Birkenhead (Woodside) and approaching Rock Ferry station with a Stephenson Locomotive Society special on 5 March 1967. *M. Dunnett*

Below right: No 92184 leaving York with an up East Coast express on 22 August 1959. *K. P. Pirt*

Above: No 92069 passing Kirby South Junction on the 'South Yorkshireman' — an unusual assignment! *J. Cupit*

Below: No 92178, minus smoke deflectors, approaching Winterbourne hauling a test train which includes the Great Western dynamometer car on 29 January 1958. *Ivo Peters*

Top right: No 92207 arriving at Newport with the 9.20am Swansea to Brockenhurst train on 27 June 1959. *S. Hodge*

Right: No 92106 at Churchdown on the Paignton-Nottingham express on 3 August 1957. *Ian Allan Library*

Below right: A '9F' banking a Bristol to Bradford train out of Bromsgrove station up the Lickey incline on 10 June 1956. Note that the locomotive is fitted with a lamp at the top of the smokebox. *A. W. Martin*

Top: Up 'Thames-Clyde Express' near Ais Gill summit on 25 June 1967 piloted by a '9F' after the Class 5 engine, working the train, failed. *W. Brian Alexander*

Above: No 92232 on the 9.5am Swansea to Kingswear train approaching Kingswear crossing on 18 July 1959. *P. F. Bowles*

Above: No 92013 passing through Skipton on a train from Edinburgh in October 1954. On the left is a 'Jubilee' class 4-6-0 on a down train.
Ian Allan Library

Left: An unidentified '9F' climbing out of Leicester Central with the 8.5am train from Bournemouth to Leeds on 27 July 1963. *G. D. King*

Below: No 92116 approaching Llandudno with a train from Crewe and overhauling an LMS Class 5 4-6-0 hauling a train from the north on the relief line, 11 June 1960. *Derek Cross*

Left: No 92122 arriving at Euston with an up Blackpool train on 5 April 1961 after the failure of Type 4 diesel locomotive No D7, which is seen behind the '9F'. *R. A. Panting*

Below left: No 92099 on the 16.48 train from Alnmouth to Alnwick on 18 June 1966; the last day of steam operation on this branch. *G. McLean*

Bottom left: No 92139 running down the gradient through Doveholes station with a Warwickshire Railway Society special from Birmingham to Doncaster on 13 November 1965. *M. S. Welch*

Top: The Severn Valley Railway and Manchester Travel Society joint railtour on 20 April 1968. The train, headed by No 92160, is joining the old Cheshire Lines at Northenden Junction. *M. Turner*

Above: Evening Star passing Barton Mill on 10 July 1977 on a special train from Scarborough to Leeds. *David Eatwell*

Left: Evening Star, once more, but this time on the type of service for which the '9Fs' were designed — passing High Wycombe on a heavy freight train from Banbury to Old Oak Common. *H. K. Harman*

Top: No 92203 recovering from a signal check at Guildford and passing the deserted MPD on the way to Cricklewood on 7 April 1968. *John H. Bird*

Above: No 92240 running through West Drayton & Yiewsley with an up freight train on 19 October 1963. *Brian Stephenson*

Top right: A heavy load for the Lickey incline: No 92155 passing through Bromsgrove on 31 May 1963 at the head of a massive train to tackle this formidable climb of two miles at 1 in 37¾. *Brian Stephenson*

Above right: No 92082 on a freight train at Harpenden in 1960. *T. A. Greaves*

Right: No 92105 with 27 wagons loaded with iron ore on the way to the north-east. *British Railways*

Right: At the end of steam in the Leeds Division: a single-chimney 2-10-0 heading south from Normanton on a tanker train in 1967.   *T. A. Greaves*

Below: A '9F' climbing Beattock with a heavy limestone train, banked by a LMS 2-6-4T engine.   *W. J. V. Anderson*

Above left: No 92015 on a mixed freight train at Elstree in 1955.
E. R. Wethersett

Left: No 92225 leaving Aberbeg with a heavy train for Ebbw Vale steel works and passing GWR '94xx' and '46xx' class 0-6-0 tank engines at the head of a returning empty train.
M. B. Rutherford

Below: No 92249 at the head of a goods train, taking water at Yeovil (Pen Mill) on 29 July 1960. *Frank Church*

Above: Evening Star crossing the River Severn at Over Junction, Gloucester, with a train of empty iron ore wagons on 2 October 1961. (Note the length of the train.) *B. V. Ashworth*

Left: No 92035 accelerating through Sandy with a fitted freight train in April 1963. *C. F. Burton*

Top right: No 92230 and GW 0-6-0 pannier tank engine No 9453 banking near the foot of the Lickey incline on 12 June 1964. *Anthony A. Vickers*

Centre right: No 92077 on a York-Manchester parcels train at Heaton Lodge Junction on 23 June 1966. *J. P. Feather*

Right: A Birmingham to Crewe freight train on the down slow line from Stafford passing Venables timber yard double-headed by '9F' No 92009 and Stanier 2-6-0 No 42950 on 22 August 1959 — a most unusual locomotive combination. *J. B. Bucknall*

4

The Class 9F Freight Engines in Service

Riddles' Standard '9Fs' must constitute one of the very few classes of locomotives which have been free from any criticism of substance. This, however, has the disadvantage that when one comes to write about them there are no troubles to discuss nor, consequently, the remedies that had to be applied to rectify them.

As we have seen, there was no immediate demand for the '9F' on account of the large number of 2-8-0 freight engines available. Even when that demand did arise there appears to have been some reluctance by the operating side to state it. P. N. Townend (who became Shed Master at King's Cross some two years after the first '9Fs' were turned out) writes:[1] 'Although it was in the Standard range, there was some delay in getting the first ones built; and eventually the Regions were asked if they really wanted such a locomotive. The Motive Power officer of the Eastern Region at the time was, I believe, L. P. Parker, who was a far-sighted and astute individual. He put pressure on to get them built, because he could see that a really good freight locomotive could run along the main line from Peterborough to Ferme Park with a good load and do the round trip in the men's eight hour day. This applied, also, elsewhere, such as the Annesley to Woodford trains, then worked by the "O1s",' Townend then refers to the LNER 'P1' class 2-8-2s of 1925, which were intended to work trains of 100 wagons, but which the traffic side could not handle. He adds that, if the 'P1s' (which were later rebuilt, like the 'A1s', with 'A3' type boilers) had survived, it might have occurred to someone to reduce their intended maximum load and increase the speed of the trains instead. This, he says, was done eventually with Class 7* freights, by providing a fitted head (ie a number of continuous brake-fitted wagons at the front) to improve the braking of the heavy coal trains and thereby increase their average speeds. The gain from the '9Fs' was not only that they were faster than the range of 2-8-0s available to the Eastern Region, but also that their time of turn-round was reduced on account of their rocker grates and hopper ashpans (which few, if any, of the 2-8-0s were modern enough to have). Townend believes that the 'K3' class 2-6-0 was tried out on fast freight trains before the arrival of the '9Fs', but with lighter loads. In his opinion: 'The "9F" turned out to be probably the best and most successful of the BR designs, as it was the only locomotive in the range that could give an improved performance beyond anything else available in the Regions.' He qualifies this statement by noting that the 'Britannias' achieved a similar success in East Anglia, where they replaced 4-6-0s which were inadequate for the services required.

The impact of the '9Fs' on freight traffic was impressive. S. C. Townroe remarks[2] that Dr (now Lord) Beeching is generally remembered for his wielding of the railway axe. However, he was continually emphasising the value of a railway system for mass transport at low cost and for the haulage of bulk loads over long distances. Whilst he was Chairman of the British Railways Board, long term contracts were sought with major industries. Of these, an early example was an agreement with the Esso Petroleum Company to carry train loads of petroleum products from the Fawley Refinery, near Southampton. In 1961 the Esso depot at Bromford Bridge, near Birmingham, began to take three train-loads of 100,000gal each every 24 hours. The weight of each train was about 1,200ton. To work them, six of the Riddles Class 9F 2-10-0s were transferred to Eastleigh motive power depot. At that time the tank wagons were still the old four-wheeled variety, used before the introduction of the bogie tank wagons, and train speeds were perforce limited to 40mph.

In order that these slow heavy trains should not interfere with passenger trains between Southampton and Basingstoke, where the track capacity had not then been improved by modern signalling, the operating authorities decided to use the Didcot, Newbury & Southampton line (now closed), despite its long single-line sections and gradients of 1 in 106. This left the main Waterloo line south of Winchester at Shawford Junction and ran to the old Great Western station at Winchester, continuing through King's Worthy and Sutton Scotney to Newbury and Didcot. The capabilities of these 2-10-0 engines were not then generally known on the Southern Region, and some pessimists predicted slipping and stalling on the heavy gradients, adding that the engines, although fitted with spark arrestors, would be certain to throw enough sparks to cause fires on these inflammable trains. None of these forecasts materialised. There were, indeed, occasional tank wagons which leaked petrol from an imperfect filler lid joint or outlet cap, but such slight leaks quickly evaporated and nothing untoward occurred. As regards the working of these trains, the '9Fs' proved masters of the job. The 'Bromfords', as the trains were known, were run consistently to time, much to the satisfaction of the Esso people. Failure on the road was almost unknown and the drivers had great confidence in their ability, with these engines, to tackle any train.

At Eastleigh there had been no occasion to call upon the '9Fs' for passenger work, but the Bournemouth and Branksome drivers, who drove them on the Somerset & Dorset line, were most enthusiastic.

The Somerset & Dorset's $71\frac{1}{2}$ miles between Bath and Bournemouth constituted one of the most difficult routes in the country. After about threequarters of a mile from the start at Bath, the line rose steeply for two miles, nearly all at 1 in 50, and entered the one-mile long Coombe Down Tunnel at the top of the ascent. Thence there followed some eight miles of severely undulating road to Radstock, which included short stretches of 1 in 60, 1 in 80, 1 in 100, and so on. Then from Radstock there was a terrific climb of $7\frac{1}{2}$ miles to the summit at Masbury, mostly at from 1 in 50 to 1 in 63. The fall from the summit on the far side was even steeper, with three miles mostly at 1 in 50 to Shepton Mallet; followed, after a short rise, by another fall at 1 in 50 for the greater part of the next four miles to Evercreech Junction. The line then undulated, with many steep rises and falls, for $34\frac{1}{2}$ miles to Corfe Mullen Junction. From there it rose at 1 in 80 for nearly two miles, and then descended for three miles through Broadstone at 1 in 97 and 1 in 76. The next two miles through Poole were level, but these were followed immediately by a final climb of two miles, much of it at 1 in 60, to Bournemouth West Junction, before dropping down for the last mile into the terminus at Bournemouth West.

Trains for Bournemouth from the north ran into the old Midland Railway terminus at Bath. Here they reversed, an engine coming on to the erstwhile rear of the train to take it on over the Somerset & Dorset section. On leaving Bath, the trains ran back for half a mile over the line they had traversed from Bristol, before bearing left at Bath Junction and curving away to the south over the old Somerset & Dorset Railway.

On 14 July 1961 that great French railway enthusiast, Baron Gerard Vuillet, rode on the footplate of the first of the Class 9Fs, No 92000 (then fitted with a double chimney), which had come on at Bath to haul the famous 'Pines Express' to Bournemouth. He describes the run in his book *Railway Reminiscences of Three Continents*.[3] The driver was D. Beale and the fireman P. Smith from Branksome Shed. Also on the footplate was Inspector Darrell Smith. Vuillet describes the weather as rainy with a south-west wind. The 'Pines Express' was loaded to 13 coaches of about 458 gross tons. It left Bath 12min 40sec late, but arrived at Bournemouth only 30sec behind time; having covered the $71\frac{1}{2}$ miles in 115min, as compared with the schedule of 130min, which included stops at Evercreech Junction, Shillingstone, Blandford Forum, Broadstone, and Poole.

Up the two miles at 1 in 50 from Bath Junction, with full regulator and cut-off advanced from 35% to 42% the engine accelerated to 24mph with boiler pressure registering 245-235lb/sq in. Over the ensuing eight mile undulating stretch to Radstock the average speed was 40mph. The climb to Masbury was started at 38mph with 32% cut-off. From there to the summit speed in mph varied over successive half miles as follows: 34, 30.3, 28.5, 24.7, 22.8, 23.9, 25.3, 30.7, 36, 34.7, 33.1, 32; with cut-offs varying from 32% to 48%, and slackening off to 23% at the approach to the summit. The regulator was full open throughout, except through the short tunnel a mile before Chilcompton, and the boiler pressure remained steady at 240lb/sq in and the water glass full. Vuillet worked out that the average equivalent drawbar horsepower for the first four miles of the ascent worked out at 2,000, with indicated horsepower at 2,240. For the entire ascent he gives the respective figures as 1,840 and 2,100. He describes this as, 'a remarkable effort indeed for a 88ton locomotive'.

Water was taken at Blandford Forum, where the water gauge showed that 3,500gal had been consumed since Bath. Six miles beyond Blandford, Bailey Gate was passed at 64mph, and the subsequent two miles of nearly level track to Corfe Mullen Junction were covered at 62mph; the speed slackening to 50mph through the junction. The 1 in 80 after Corfe Mullen Junction was climbed without speed dropping below 43mph, with full regulator and 45% cut-off. Before Poole, the train was brought to a stand for one minute by the passage of a Weymouth boat train on the Southern Region main line. A mile beyond Poole the last ascent began. Vuillet describes the traverse of this stretch as follows: 'With full regulator and 49% cut-off, a speed of 47mph was achieved at the foot of the gradient, and then, with cut-off advanced to 52% through Parkstone — with a terrific roar — the summit was passed at 41mph, the 2.5 miles from Poole having been covered in 4min 20sec. On the gradient the boiler pressure was 225lb/sq in. As the line changes its course to the east of Poole, the wind was now helping us. This and the shortness of the run makes an estimate of the developed horsepower difficult, but calculations point to the possibility of an indicated horsepower of 2,800 during one minute.'

Another trip on a '9F' hauling the 'Pines Express' was recorded by R. Nelson.[4] The load was again 12 coaches, weighing 440 tons full, and the driver and fireman were again D. C. Beale and P. Smith, respectively, while Inspector Evans was also on the footplate. The engine was No 92233, another of those fitted with a double chimney. Nelson had come up on the 11.40am train from Bournemouth to Bath, travelling on the footplate of Riddles Class 4 4-6-0 No 75027, hauling a light train of 155ton full. It is a tribute to the design of the Riddles engines in general that, of the seven-mile steep ascent to Masbury from Evercreech Junction, Nelson remarks: 'I was interested to note that at full regulator the boiler and steam chest pressure gauges gave identical readings, speaking volumes for the care given to the design of the internal steam passages.' (It is of some minor interest that No 75027 is now preserved on the Bluebell Railway, and that I rode on the footplate when I was invited to commission the engine on to that line in the unfortunate absence in hospital of Mr Riddles.) However, it was unfortunate for the recording of '9F' performance that the Class 4 4-6-0 was engaged on an unbalanced working, and it was the practice at that time to return it to Evercreech Junction as pilot on the 'Pines Express'. From there to Blandford, as Nelson says, there were no gradients requiring hard workings, but he noted that the engine was linked up to 10% cut-off. He was most impressed with the riding qualities of the 2-10-0 with its 5ft coupled wheels. The climb from Corfe Mullen Junction was surmounted at $39\frac{3}{4}$mph with 45% cut-off and full regulator. The final opportunity to see what the engine could do came with the 1 in 60 of Parkstone Bank after restarting from Poole. Nelson writes: 'It was traditional to go hard here, since no one cared if the fire was torn to pieces when the engine was just coming off at Bournemouth West. Station overtime had left us 2min behind time at this point and Donald Beale set out with a vengeance to recover it if he could in these last 4½ miles. So after a deceptively gentle start — due to restrictions over the level crossings outside the station — he opened out to full regulator, first with 35, then 45, and finally 55% cut-off! This was not merely rousing the echoes; it was maintaining a steady 41½mph up 1 in 60 with 440 tons. I calculate the equivalent drawbar horsepower here to be 2,439 — considerably the highest I have ever known with steam.' The summit was passed in about the same time as on Vuillet's run, and Nelson's edhp of 2,439 would suggest perhaps a roughly similar ihp to Vuillet's estimate of 2,800.

Both the above trips describe the use of these engines on express passenger workings — a use for which, of course, they were never intended; not even for such a difficult route as the Somerset & Dorset. However, in view of their success on the S&D trains, it is a pity that they were never tried on passenger trains over the old Highland Railway main line between Perth and Inverness. In connection with this, Riddles believed that he was mistaken in designing the Class 6 'Clans' as 4-6-2s instead of 4-8-0s;[5] because the latter wheel arrangement would have been far better for general use in Scotland, giving greater adhesion whilst providing for the frequent tender-first working. At the time the remarkable adaptability of the '9F' 2-10-0s could not have been foretold, but with the addition of these two types all Scottish locomotive requirements could probably have been met.

Soon after their first appearance, the '9Fs' were found to be fast runners and inevitably found their way on to the excursion and relief passenger trains. The speed they could develop on these tasks was brought to public notice in an unusual way through an often quoted account in the 14 December 1955 issue of the weekly magazine *The Motor*. The occasion was a demonstration run by an Alvis car from Coventry to Glasgow. On the A76 road running north from Dumfries the car was travelling alongside the main line of the old Glasgow & South Western Railway connecting Carlisle and Glasgow. Ahead of them the driver and his companion saw a passenger train which they began to overhaul. They wrote: 'We began to overtake coach by coach a 14-coach express hauled by a big black brute of a locomotive with numerous massive driving wheels. Soon both driver and fireman had spotted us and were leaning out of the cab window and waving us on, a challenge which we met by urging the speedometer needle up into the "80s".' The passenger in the car took a photograph of the engine which showed it to be No 92023, built in May 1955 and one of the 10 fitted with a Franco-Crosti boiler (discussed in the next chapter).

The very last steam locomotive to be built for British Railways was Class 9F No 92220, completed at Swindon

in March 1960. At a special ceremony at Swindon it was named *Evening Star* by K. W. C. Grand, Member of the British Transport Commission and a former Chief Regional Officer of the Western Region of British Railways. The name was singularly appropriate for the last engine because Stephenson's 'Star' class were the first successful locomotives to be built for the old broad gauge Great Western Railway, and one of them had been named *Morning Star*. The engine was beautifully turned out by Swindon in the old Great Western livery, complete with copper-capped double chimney. Presiding over the ceremony was that eminent Great Western enthusiast, my friend the late R. F. Hanks. He had been trained on the GWR and, after leaving the company for a distinguished career in Morris Motors, had returned as Chairman of Western Area Board, BTC. He said of the *Evening Star* that the engine was not of the Great Western breed, but that they had done their best to make up for that 'by dollying her up in good old Western colours and by conferring on her the finest honour we can — the halo or crown of Swindon, the copper top to her chimney'. Hanks told me that the whole affair, including copper chimney top, had been arranged by him. His own Oxford garden was adorned with Great Western mementos, including the chimney and name plate from a locomotive and whistles surmounting the gate posts. However, Hanks was not on very firm historical ground as regards chimneys; for his hero, G. J. Churchward, was quite happy with the plain tapered cast iron chimneys which adorned many of his locomotives. Riddles, a London & North Western man by upbringing, was not particularly pleased with the Great Western 'look' applied to one of his engines, but by this time he had retired from the railway. There had been an earlier attempt to export the Swindon chimney. As part of his plan to wean the various Locomotive Works away from practices of the old companies that conflicted with the common standards which he was trying to establish, Riddles cross-posted Regional Mechanical Engineers. Doncaster, thus, found itself subjected to Swindon influence, and a Class V2 2-6-2 suddenly sprouted a Great Western copper-capped chimney. The railway exchanges of 1925 between a GWR 'Castle' and a LNER Pacific were still remembered at Doncaster, and Riddles was horrified when the information reached him. He directed Bond to order the immediate removal of the offending chimney.

Evening Star played a notable part in displaying the versatility of the '9Fs'. When new it was allocated to Cardiff Canton shed, and for a time worked Cardiff-Portsmouth passenger trains as far as Salisbury and back. On 27 June 1960 the engine was waiting at Cardiff to work its Portsmouth train, when the 'Britannia' allocated to haul the up 'Red Dragon' express failed. Driver E. Broom, who was to have driven the 'Britannia', agreed to take over the 2-10-0, presumably with some reluctance; but, if so, any anxiety was soon dissipated. The 'Red Dragon' was loaded to 13 coaches weighing 450 tons full. With the engine working at from 16% to 17% cut-off on level sections. Broom reported an excellent run on both the up and following down expresses. The '9Fs' did not have a speedometer, but he thought that a maximum

58

speed of 80 to 85mph was reached on the down train over the falling gradients approaching the Severn Tunnel. After this successful debut, *Evening Star* worked the 'Red Dragon' and 'Capitals United' expresses from Cardiff to Paddington and back on 28 and 29 June and on 1 and 5 July.[6] Nemesis came after the driver had to stop at Reading for water, because a preceding train had emptied the Goring troughs, and the '9Fs' were heavy on water. Paddington promptly banned the use of *Evening Star* on crack expresses, and she reverted to her normal working of either Cardiff to Salisbury and back, or to Hereford with oil tanks.[7]

The most notable high speed run by a '9F' has been described by P. N. Townend and T. A. Greaves (the latter, at the time of writing, being British Railways' Traction and Train Crew Manager).[8]

On summer Saturdays the depot at Kings Cross was given a considerable number of additional diagrams for Pacifics and 'V2s', well beyond those which could be worked by the engines allocated. A number of Kings Cross engines were not available on Saturdays until the afternoon because they had gone down on Friday lodging turns. The first one of these to return was on train No 971 up from Leeds, due at 1.40pm, having worked the down 'Yorkshire Pullman' the previous day. Everything at the depot was sent out on these summer Saturday mornings, including any 'foreign' locomotives on hand, 'but', says Townend, 'by 1.45pm the depot was generally "Knocking"'. This particular occasion was, he says, 'the only time that I ever saw the running shed completely empty of locomotives.' It had been a problem to find an engine for the 1.45pm to Grantham, a slow train of five coaches. Greaves adds that soon after 2pm sufficient 'up-road' locomotives could be serviced and allocated to the afternoon trains. For the 1.45, he continues: 'The alternatives were one of the "9Fs", which Peter Townend the permanent shed master had groomed for main line service, following running in on the Cambridge expresses, and an "off-beat wonder", a Doncaster "V2" in a run-down condition. Driver Baur opted for the "9F".' This was one of the double-chimney 2-10-0s.

The '9F' was accordingly sent down on the 'slow' and Grantham was asked to replace it with something more suitable to work the up 'Heart of Midlothian' (for which Grantham was responsible for providing the engine) to Kings Cross. Greaves says that the driver 'kept running time to Grantham without difficulty, and I then thought the problems were over as Grantham had a Kings Cross 'A4' unbalanced for the return working. Unfortunately they had used it for a northbound train and the driver was given the Class 9 to return. What had not been appreciated was that the General Manager had been to Colwick to open the Railway Sports, and that his saloon was attached to the back of the London bound train. After hitting 92 down the Stoke bank, the VIP party paused at Kings Cross to congratulate the driver on a good run. To their surprise they found a "9F" at the buffer stops in place of an "A4" or an "A1". Later that evening the telephone line started to buzz. When the driver was interviewed he was told that he was expected to keep time — not break the bloody sound barrier; to which he laugh-

ingly replied: "We just gave her her head and she ran like a dream."'

Townend adds: 'On the Monday following some questions were asked of the Running Officer by the General Manager about the suitability of using a freight locomotive on crack expresses, and someone asked me what the speed limit was. Of course the reply was that there was generally no speed restriction on the locomotive but the track or the particular category of the train determined the maximum speed. I had to say that the driver had not exceeded any restriction and could not therefore be criticised. It was then decided that a restriction should be put on locomotives equal to the diameter of the driving wheels in inches. When put to me I pointed out that all the Pacifics would be, in consequence, limited to 74-80mph which would not help punctuality; so no more was said. Subsequently we very occasionally used a "9F" on this turn on Saturdays, when desperate, but no one worried further.'

Greaves, some two years after this incident, was travelling from Sheffield to a meeting in London. He says:[9] 'A Sulzer Crompton Parkinson (Class 45 2,500hp diesel-electric locomotive) failed at Wellingborough and I went forward to find a coolant hose had burst, resulting in an engine shut-down. The relays were manipulated and we got the locomotive off the train, to be given a filthy run-down Class 9 of the single chimney variety. We had a "green fire" with barely 120lb/sq in on the clock, so after blacking out Wellingborough with a smoke screen and getting clear signals following the passing of the Pullman, we took off towards St Pancras. Harry Strafford, the driver, had never had a "9F", so he was advised to put the regulator in the roof and wind it down until she slipped. He took the GN driving style to heart, and with both the fireman and myself (dressed in a fireman's oiling up overalls, which had been borrowed) firing, we managed to get steam back, although we hardly saw the water until we reached Saviour Summit. But this Class 9 ran like a Banshee and we kept diesel timings to Dock Junction, where the regulator was closed for the first time. The racket from the big-end had to be heard to be believed, but as an Eastern man I had little sympathy for the Midland if they could not look after their locos better.

'The story did not end there, however, I entered the office of the Assistant Line Engineer, feeling that I had done a good day's work before the meeting started, only to be blasted for leaving a set of oily coal black footprints across his then new carpet! In those days one could not win!'

Greaves concludes: 'In the Leeds and Sheffield Division, towards the end of steam, the "9F", irrespective of maintenance standard, was always master of the job. Providing one was not too gentle and the fireman was able to get coal into the back corners, there was not a freight locomotive to equal it. My opinion is that the "9Fs" and the Austerities were the most outstanding of Mr Riddles' designs. Provided that the tyres were kept in good order and the boiler washed out regularly, the WD locomotives would run on almost zero maintenance. The impression amongst many people that the Austerity was light on its feet was invariably caused by poor tyre condition, due to extended shopping cycles prevailing before the locomotives were withdrawn.'

Notes
1 P. N. Townend, in a letter to the Author
2 S. C. Townroe, letter to the Author
3 Gerard Vuillet, *Railway Reminiscences in Three Continents* (London, Nelson, 1958), pp281-4
4 R. Nelson, *Locomotive Performance* (London, Ian Allan, 1979), pp124-5
5 R. A. Riddles, information to the Author
6 E. S. Cox, *Standard Steam Locomotives* (London, Ian Allan, 1966), p168
7 D. S. Barrie, letter to the Author
8 P. N. Townend and T. A. Greaves, letters to the Author
9 T. A. Greaves, letter to the Author

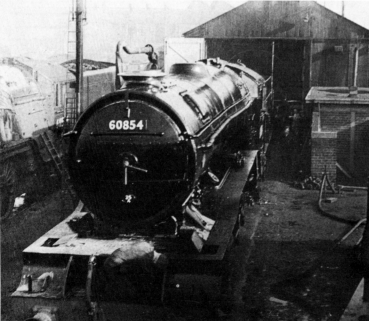

Above: No 92223 heading a Preston bound freight train south from Carnforth on 12 August 1967. *C. J. Mills*

Left: A Great Western appearance at Doncaster. The type of copper-capped double chimney which adorned *Evening Star*; but here it decorates LNER 'V2' class 2-6-2 No 60854. Riddles ordered its immediate removal, and this is believed to be the only photograph of No 60854 with its temporary embellishment. *T. A. Greaves*

Above right: An impressive spectacle, as No 92093 surges up the bank from Preston with an up freight train. *J. H. Cooper-Smith*

Right: No 92077 piloting Stanier Class 5 4-6-0 and climbing out of Hellifield with an oil train from Heysham to Leeds on 11 March 1967. *Maurice S. Burns*

Above: No 92114 with a train of empty wagons passing one of Robinson's famous Great Central 2-8-0 locomotives on an Ordsall Lane to Ardwick goods train at Manchester Exchange, August 1960. *J. R. Carter*

Right: No 92244 passing Stoke Gifford sidings with a coal train on 23 April 1959. *B. A. Poley*

Below right: No 92213 climbing Hatton Bank with empties for Bordesley Yard, Birmingham. *K. R. Pirt*

Above right: No 92137 leaving the spur from the Nuneaton line Wigston Magna station on 3 June 1961. *A. Mensing*

Right: No 92082 hauling an up freight train through Malton station on 29 September 1962. *M. Pope*

Below: No 92231 with a train of Esso tankers leaving Bromsgrove yard to ascend the Lickey incline on 26 October 1961. *A. Davenport*

Top left: No 92019, on an oil train, waiting in the loop at Grayrigg, whilst being overtaken by a down parcels train headed by a 'Britannia' class Pacific No 70025. *Ivo Peters*

Left: No 92014 on a long freight train at Trumpington in 1954. *E. R. Wethersett*

Below left: No 92186 leaving Peterborough on a parcels train and climbing to the Nene bridge. *P. N. Townend*

Above: No 92151 passing Ashchurch with a southbound freight train. On the right the 4.30pm train for Redditch is waiting to depart behind Ivatt '4F' class 2-6-0 No 43047, travelling tender first. *R. E. James-Robertson*

Below: No 92160 on a freight train near Harpenden. *T. A. Greaves*

Left: No 92118 starting a south-bound freight train from Normanton. *T. A. Greaves*

Below: No 92104 with a Carlisle to Stourton freight train passing Ivatt Class 4 2-6-0 in the yard at Wortley Junction, Leeds. *G. W. Morrison*

Top: No 92147 at Peterborough North with an up freight train. *P. H. Wells*

Above: Preserved '9F' No 92203 *Black Prince* in immaculate condition heading a train of goods wagons at Cranmore in 1981. *R. O. Coffin*

Left: No 92189 approaching the Dearness Valley signalbox on 30 July 1961 with an up freight train, diverted via Bishop Auckland because of engineering work on the main line. The locomotive is about to cross over the trailing connection from the Blackhill line, and then the facing connection for the Waterhouses branch, which diverges to the right; the whole forming an attractive track layout. *I. S. Carr*

Left: No 92010 on a freight train at Broxbourne in 1955. *E. R. Wethersett*

Below: No 92203 on the last steam-hauled Bidston (Birkenhead) to Summers Steel Works train at Shotton on 6 June 1967, with Sir Richard Summers at the regulator. *E. N. Knede*

Tyne Dock-Consett

Right: No 92062 starting its train load of iron ore for the Consett Works from under the ore bunkers at Tyne Dock. The white discs above each track show that a complete set of hoppers are charged and ready to load a train of the specially constructed ore wagons, all of which were loaded simultaneously in a few seconds. The reverse side of these discs were painted black to show that the hoppers were not ready for discharging. Two Westinghouse compressors can be seen on the engine. These are to maintain a pressure to keep the wagon doors closed and also to operate the mechanism to open the doors for unloading. *Charles H. Dean*

Below right: The guard of a Tyne Dock to Consett iron ore train waiting to couple up the banking engine, No 92099, at South Pelaw on 27 May 1964. *M Dunnett*

Above: Two '9Fs', Nos 92061 and 92062, with an iron ore train of nine wagons, climbing a gradient of 1 in 56, to be followed by even steeper gradients of up to 1 in 35. The train has just left the Pontop and South Shields branch along which it has been travelling since shortly after leaving Tyne Docks. It now follows the Blackhill line towards Consett Iron Works, while ahead the Pontop and South Shields branch diverges to the left to Stella Gill. *Charles H. Dean*

Right: No 92062 blowing off steam at the head of the iron ore train whilst climbing the 1 in 54 to Annfield East where the gradient steepens to 1 in 35. On this occasion the banker was an '01' class 2-8-0 No 63712 instead of a '9F'. *Charles H. Dean*

Below right: With No 92064 leading and stoker-fitted No 92167 banking, the iron ore train ascends the 1 in 35 gradient between Stanley and Annfield Plain on 14 August 1962. *J. M. Rayner*

Above: No 92097, with another '9F' banking, rounding the bend past Pelton village with a Consett iron ore train in June 1964. *M. Dunnett*

Left: No 92060 hauling the iron ore train, assisted by another '9F' as banker up the 1 in 49 gradient between Pelton and Beamish on 15 May 1964. *Verdun Wake*

Below left: No 92063 climbing through Beamish with the last steam Tyne Dock to Consett iron ore train on 19 November 1966. *M. Dunnett*

Above: The iron ore train near Leadgate with No 92063 at the head and '01' class 2-8-0 No 63760 banking on 27 June 1962. *M. Dunnett*

Left: The last steam-hauled iron ore train, headed by No 92063, discharging the iron ore hoppers on the unloading gantry at Consett Steel Works on 19 November 1966. *John R. P. Hunt*

Below left: No 92060 at South Pelaw Junction with the empty iron ore wagons on the way to Tyne Dock. The detached banker, '01' class 2-8-0 No 63712, is waiting to bank the next train to Consett. *Charles H. Dean*

Top: A single chimney '9F' class 2-10-0 No 92034 at the New England Depot. This was one of the earlier engines, built in December 1954 and allocated immediately to New England. *P. N. Townend*

Above: No 92040 with a single chimney at Borrow Hill MPD in the Sheffield Division. *T. A. Greaves*

Above left: Single chimney No 92038 in the early 1960s, engaged on the High Munckton power station workings. Note the flangeless centre coupled wheels. *T. A. Greaves*

Left: Single chimney No 92113, built November 1956. *T. A. Greaves*

Above: Single chimney No 92148 at New England Depot. Note the immaculate turnout. *P. N. Townend*

Right: The first '9F' to be fitted with a double chimney; No 92178 at Swindon on 8 September 1957, newly turned out from the works. *G. W. Morrison*

Right: Double chimney No 92196 in steam at Kings Cross Top Shed. This engine was kept especially groomed for Great Northern main line passenger working. *T. A. Greaves*

Below: Another engine, No 92202, showing the high standard of turnout at Kings Cross Top Shed. *P. N. Townend*

Bottom: Nose-to-nose at Holbeck: single and double chimney '9F' 2-10-0s. *T. A. Greaves*

Top right: No 92217 bearing a legend justified perhaps by the speed exploits of these locomotives, but amended by, apparently, someone who just does not believe the stories! *Cecil J. Blay*

Centre right: No 92207 with double chimney, turned out magnificently at Swindon. *J. B. Bucknall*

Right: The first double-chimney '9F', No 92178, as operating in the Great Northern suburban area. This presents a good view of the flangeless centre coupled wheels. Note the access hole in the cab side sheet. *T. A. Greaves*

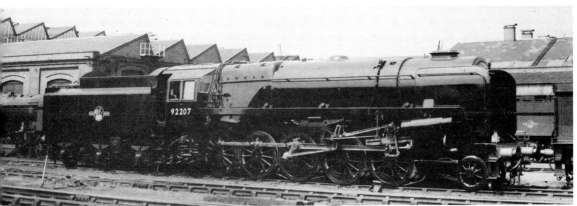

Right: No 92012 running on to the turntable at Leeds Holbeck past an immaculate 'B1' 4-6-0 No 61306 on 23 September 1967. *John A. M. Vaughan*

Below: No 92234 backing into Birkenhead (Woodside) to work a Stephenson Locomotive Society special, watched by a keen observer on the platform. In the foreground is the station pilot, Stanier 2-6-4T engine No 42616. 5 March 1967. *M. Dunnett*

Above: Preserved '9F' No 92203 *Black Prince* at Eastleigh Open Day on 26 March 1972. *N. E. Preedy*

Left: No 92012 again on the turntable at Leeds Holbeck, and between ill-assorted companions! 23 September 1967. *John A. M. Vaughan*

Below left: Crewe South Shed on 23 April 1965 with No 92110 and 'Britannia' class Pacifics Nos 70022 and 70013. *D. Percival*

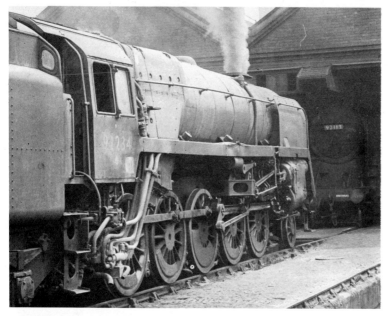

Above left: A very mixed bag at Weymouth in 1962, with No 92128, Riddles Class 4 4-6-0 No 75064, and other British Railways and Great Western engines. *D. H. Cape*

Left: Banbury Depot on 1 July 1966, showing Nos 92234 and 92113. The latter is about to work a southbound freight train. *Ian Allan Library*

Below: York Motive Power Depot on 1 May 1966, with No 92137 accompanied by LNER 'V2' class 2-6-2 No 60824 and a 'B1' class 4-6-0. *P. Hocquard*

Above left: Carlisle Kingmoor running shed on 24 May 1967, with, from left to right, No 92004, 'Britannia' Class No 70032 *Tennyson*, No 92129, Stanier 2-8-0 No 48283, and 'Britannia' class No 70039 *Sir Christopher Wren*. *J. L. McIvor*

Left: Swindon on 12 April 1964, showing No 92222, GWR '94xx' class 0-6-0 tank engine No 9430, and Stanier Class 5F 2-6-0 No 42983. *Ian Allan Library*

Below: The arrival of No 92212 on 17 February 1980 at Loughborough for preservation. Inside the shed is No 71000 *Duke of Gloucester*. Track has been laid at the rear of the shed to receive the '9F' and the back wall has been removed so that it can be moved into covered accommodation. *Graham Wignall*

5
Construction and Modifications

Having described some of the outstanding performances of the '9F' class in traffic, it is time to turn to the details of design and construction which contributed so effectively to these performances and to the largely ineffective attempts to improve their efficiency.

The leading dimensions and other factors of these remarkable engines were as follows:

Cylinders (2), diameter and stroke   20in by 28in
Wheels:
   Coupled, diameter   5ft
   Pony Truck, diameter   3ft
   Tender, diameter   3ft $3\frac{1}{2}$in
Wheelbase:
   Coupled   21ft 8in
   Engine   30ft 2in
   Engine and Tender   55ft 11in
Heating Surface:
   Tubes   1,836sq ft
   Firebox   179sq ft
   Total Evaporative   2,015sq ft
   Superheater   535sq ft
Grate Area: 40.2sq ft
Boiler Pressure: 250lb/sq in
Tractive Effort: 39,667lb
Adhesion Factor: 4.38
Weight of Engine in Working Order: 86ton 14cwt
Weight of Engine and Tender in Working Order:
139ton 4cwt

The basic diagram of the engine was worked out by the Derby Drawing Office and then handed over to the Brighton Drawing Office to which the detailed design had been allocated, following their completion of the drawings for the Class 4 4-6-0s and 2-6-0s. The design project did not entail any special problems other than the boiler (discussed in Chapter 3). In order to provide a large enough boiler and firebox to fit within the height limits imposed by the 5ft coupled wheels, considerable departure had to be made from the 'Britannia' design; and in fact a completely new boiler was designed with the ashpan and grate tailored to the minimal height necessary for effective operation.[1]

It is worth noting that the basic design had been worked out so well in the Development Drawing Office at Derby, that in all the subsequent work at Brighton on detailed design, no departure was found necessary or desirable from this basic scheme. Nevertheless, or course, many items had to be worked out and minor problems dealt with as the job proceeded.[2]

Because the firebox was shallower than in the Pacifics, it was necessary to incorporate a firegrate in which the rear portion was horizontal and the front part sloping. The grate was a rocking type with 12 rocking sections, each section having 12 grid firebars. It was divided longitudinally so that each side could be rocked independently. When, from the footplate, the gear was put to full travel, the fire could be dropped, as required, for instance, when standing over a pit; whilst a limited movement of the rocking sections, whilst running, would break up clinker and eliminate ash. The ashpan was self-emptying, with two hopper doors at its base between the frames. The airflow to the grate was regulated by front and rear damper doors.

Below: The Class 9F 2-10-0 as built.

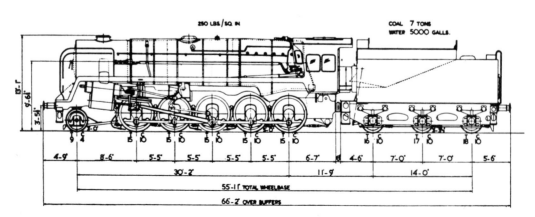

When the first locomotive was sent to work in the South Wales area, a problem arose over slipping whilst hauling heavy iron ore trains from Rogerstone to Ebbw Vale, and difficulty over closing the regulator. In order to save weight it had been decided to fit a regulator based on the type used on the LMS rather than that adopted for the 'Britannias'. The slipping occurred when the regulator was opened a little too far, so that the main valve just cracked. If the engine slipped, the driver would try to close the regulator; but whilst the pilot valve closed the main valve remained slightly open, allowing sufficient steam to flow for the slipping to persist. The reason for this was that, with the wheels slipping freely, the steam passed through the cylinders without producing any back pressure at the regulator, so that its main valve was locked on its seating by the boiler pressure, and consequently immovable. The solution found was to apply the brakes, thus slowing down the rotation and hence the flow of steam through the cylinders. Back pressure then built up in the steam pipe, equalising the pressure below and above the main valve, which could then be closed. The regulator was consequently re-designed after the first batch had been built.[3]

The smokebox was provided with self-cleaning apparatus, consisting of a nearly vertical plate in front of the tubes and a horizontal plate, so as to conduct the gases downward and to the front of the smokebox. A wire gauze screen was placed across the gas passage to the chimney which prevented the emission of large particles of unburnt fuel.

The frames were very robust, comprising $1\frac{1}{4}$in thick frame plates. Riddles never contemplated using bar frames, as in American practice, because they would not have allowed the slight flexing which was necessary for the long coupled wheel base.[4]

Plain bearing axle boxes were used throughout the engine. The coupled wheel axle boxes were steel castings with bearings consisting of pressed-in horse shoe brass lined with white metal. The tyres of the five pairs of coupled wheels were secured to the cast steel centres by Gibson rings. Steam sanding was provided to the leading and driving coupled wheels for running in the forward direction, and to the driving wheels only for reverse running. The driving, or centre, pair of coupled wheels were flangeless.

The piston valves reflected the Churchward doctrine with their maximum travel of $7\frac{7}{8}$in, steam lap of $1\frac{11}{16}$in, and lead of $\frac{1}{4}$in.

In order to obtain the widest possible route availability from the Chief Civil Engineer, it was necessary to keep the coupled wheel axle loads down to 15ton 10cwt, which entailed very close attention to detail weights throughout the locomotive. In addition, the hammer blow, resulting from the vertical component of the reciprocating masses (ie piston heads, rods, crossheads, and part of the connecting rods) needed to be kept to a minimum. This was achieved by adapting a feature used in the Bulleid Pacifics. In connection with the Southern Railway three-cylinder 'Schools' class locomotives, H. Holcroft had suggested to Bulleid that counter-balancing reciprocating parts on a three-cylinder locomotive was unnecessary because the longitudinal forces were self-balanced, and the weight was only added to offset the couples set up by the forces working in different planes. If all reciprocating balance were omitted it would result in the abolition of hammer blow on the rails. He proposed that the theory should be tried out on one of the 'Schools' class three-cylinder 4-4-0s. Bulleid accepted this, and balance weights on one of these engines were cut down so that they balanced rotating parts only. The Locomotive Testing Section reported that the riding was no different from others of the class, and that wear, after a period, was unaffected. No more 'Schools' were altered, but the experiment led to the omission of all reciprocating balance from Bulleid's Pacifics, with consequent absence of hammer blow. It was considered that the principle could be applied to a two-cylinder engine of comparable size, such as the 2-10-0, if the reciprocating masses of the latter were force-balanced only and not couple-balanced. This meant that, while the rotating masses were completely balanced within the large lead balance weights in the coupled wheels, the weights to balance the reciprocating masses were located at the same angle in both wheels of each pair, whereby a smaller quantity of lead was necessary. This reduced the hammer blow, unsprung weight, and overall weight. The efficiency of the balancing system was proved by the remarkably smooth performance of these 5ft wheel engines when, coming to the rescue of hard-pressed depots, they hauled express trains at speeds which at times exceeded 90mph.[5]

Some minor alterations to the '9Fs' were made by BR Regions. For instance, when first allocated to Eastern Region's New England Depot, the fittings in the cab were made to LNER standards in order to make them more acceptable to the men, and LNER firehole doors were fitted for the same reason. But the only problem that arose related to the brick arch; for it had a very short life of usually only a few weeks. This was due, no doubt, to the very shallow wide firebox. P. N. Townend was asked to look into this and discovered that the London Midland Region were putting in concrete arches at their Wellingborough Depot. He accordingly went there and borrowed a set of the formers required. Concrete arches were then installed in the '9Fs' at New England, and proved so successful that the Eastern Region adopted them as standard. The concrete arches lasted for the six months between boiler inspections, when the arch had to be removed anyway. A special cement was obtained from Falkirk in Scotland and used with crushed firebrick aggregate. The only drawback was that it required curing for a minimum of 12 hours before the engine could be lit up, but this loss of availability was more than made up by the extended life of the arch.[6]

As an instance of the high appreciation with which the '9Fs' were regarded, Townend says that: 'No 92196, a Doncaster locomotive, was exhibited at the Noel Park Exhibition held to commemorate the 750th Anniversary of Wood Green Charter. There was a mass of copper pipes on the right hand side which my chargehand cleaner polished.'

There was a major, and very interesting, modification to the '9Fs', following a decision to build 10 of them with a Crosti boiler. This device had been invented by an eminent Italian engineer, Piero Crosti of Milan. It had been fitted to a number of Italian locomotives (2-6-0s, 2-6-2s, and 2-8-0s) and also to many German ones. In the two countries, in fact, some 130 locomotives were reported to have shown an economy of more than 20% in fuel consumption after rebuilding with Crosti boilers. This saving was effected mainly by using the heat which in a conventional steam locomotive was wasted to the atmosphere through the chimney.

In the Crosti system used in Italy and Germany, two subsidiary boilers were placed on either side of the normal boiler barrel. These subsidiary boilers were preheaters through which the gases from the flue tubes passed to two chimneys immediately in front of the cab.

Owing to the restrictions of the British loading gauge, it was not possible to accommodate these two subsidiary boilers, or drums, on either side of the boiler proper, and a modification had therefore to be devised. Instead of two preheater drums, there was only one, and this was placed between the frames and underneath the boiler barrel, with the centre line of the drum sloping downwards towards the rear.

Essentially, the Crosti boiler was a form of feedwater heater; the function of the drum being to heat the feed water so that it entered the boiler at a temperature only slightly less than that of the water already there. The drum had a final smokebox located just in front of the throat plate of the main boiler, and the blast chamber and final chimney were on the right hand side of the boiler barrel, just ahead of the firebox.

In addition to the flue tube gases, some heat was extracted from a portion of the steam exhausted through the left hand cylinder exhaust pipe, which portion was fed into a jacket encircling part of the preheater drum. The remaining exhaust steam, from both cylinners, passed to the rear smokebox. Exhaust steam could also be used in an exhaust steam injector.

The water circuit was as follows: the cold feed from the tender was forced through a clack valve at the rear end of the preheater drum, either by an exhaust steam injector or by a feed pump; the water in the preheater, displaced by the entry of this fresh feed, moved forward and eventually passed through pipes to the main boiler clack valves; the hot gases and the cold feed thus flowing in opposite directions.

The boiler of the Crosti 2-10-0 was smaller in diameter than that of the standard '9Fs', but was otherwise similar in principle. There was a chimney in the normal position, but this was only used for lighting up and was closed for normal running. However, a chimney in the traditional position plays an important part in the appearance of a steam locomotive, so that the '9F' Crostis, compared to their Italian 'cousins', were quite pleasant to look at.

There was a superheater header of normal design in the front smokebox. The exhaust steam from the cylinders, instead of passing into the base of a blast pipe in the front smokebox, was carried back in two long pipes, of which that from the right hand cylinder went directly to the blast chamber, and that from the left hand cylinder passed back on that side and then under the boiler barrel to join the right hand pipe before entering the blast chamber and thence the multiple jet blast pipe.

Dimensions of the Crosti engines differed from the standard '9Fs' as follows:

Heating Surface:
   Main Boiler Tubes 1,274sq ft
   Firebox 158sq ft
   Total Evaporative 1,432sq ft
   Superheater 411sq ft
   Preheater Tubes 1,021sq ft
   Exhaust Steam Jacket 57sq ft
Weight of Engine in Working Order: 90ton 4cwt
Weight of Engine & Tender in Working Order: 141ton 9cwt

Below: Diagram of Franco Crosti boiler as fitted to the '9Fs'.

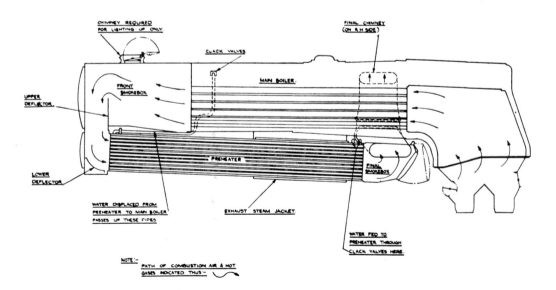

84

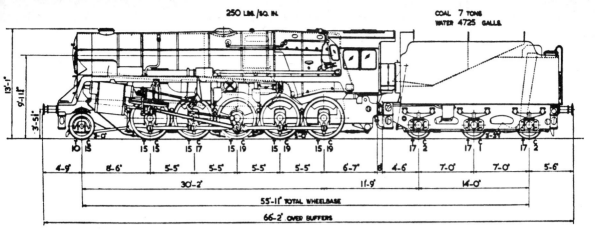

Above: Diagram of the '9Fs' fitted with Crosti boilers.

The 10 Crosti engines were turned out in 1955, and a series of tests were carried out at Rugby and on the line between Crosti engine No 92023 and standard '9F' No 92050. It had been agreed that the royalty to be paid to the Italian Franco Company should be the agreed amount if the Crosti engine showed savings of at least 18%, but that no royalties at all would be paid if the savings were only 12% or below. Savings between these two figures would be at the agreed ratio. In fact the results of the tests showed savings far below 12%. In addition, as had happened so often with tubular heaters in the past, such savings on fuel costs as there were, were more than offset by increased maintenance charges. There was an additional disadvantage in that, whilst the standard '9Fs' were splendid engines to ride on, the Crostis were very unpleasant because the smoke and steam from the chimney, which was just outside the fireman's side of the cab, swirled all round the footplate. Owing to the failure of the tests to show adequate savings, therefore, it was not long before the preheater drums were removed and the Crosti '9Fs' altered for normal working — though they retained the smaller diameter boilers and distinctive appearance.

After the results of the tests had been made known and had been accepted by Dr Crosti himself and the adjudicator from the Italian State Railways testing staff (both of whom had been at Rugby during the tests), the Italian Franco Company asked if they could be scrutinised by an independent authority. British Railways, having agreed to this request, the relevant data were sent to the eminent French steam locomotive engineer, M. André Chapelon. After some delay, due to his illness, Chapelon submitted a masterly analysis to British Railways, which R. C. Bond, as CME, sent on to D. R. Carling, who had conducted the tests at Rugby, for comment. Carling was delighted at Chapelon's assessment of the tests as 'the most consistent and accurate in his experience'. Such a tribute from one of the greatest exponents of steam locomotive testing was regarded by Carling as a complete vindication of the work of his staff at Rugby and also of the Derby team who had carried out the tests on the line.[7]

There were several reasons for the failure to attain the economy expected. Firstly, there had been a misunderstanding between Crosti and BR's representative at the initial discussions (which were carried out in French — a language native to neither of them). Crosti's claim to the percentage greater economy of his system over conventional Italian locomotives was based, however, not only on the arrangement described above, but included a feedwater heater *additional* to that provided by the preheater drums. Perhaps due to language difficulties, he failed to make it clear that his comparative figures had been obtained from tests between an engine fitted with a Crosti boiler *and* feedwater heater, and one which had neither. He was told that BR locomotives did not use feedwater heaters but did have exhaust steam injectors. Crosti accepted the use of exhaust steam injector in place of a feedwater heater, but did not, apparently, appreciate that the standard '9F', with which the Crosti '9F' was to be compared, *would* have an exhaust steam injector as part of its normal equipment.[8]

An exhaust steam injector, in steady running, produces a reduction in feedwater consumption for the same power output of about 6%. This is made up of an actual saving of about 8%, for the same amount of steam, less an increase in steam consumption of about 2% because of reduced superheat. This would lower an expected saving of 10% by the Crosti to 4%. In addition, there were two other factors, neither of which were inherent to the Crosti system. Chapelon's analysis showed that the '9F' Crosti boiler was slightly more scaled than that of the standard '9F', although both were almost new out of Crewe Works. Examination of the feedwater records at Rugby revealed no reason for this difference, though it would result in a further reduction in the percentage saving, possibly in the region of 1% or 2%. The other factor, which has never yet been explained, was that the Crosti engine had an appreciably greater resistance to movement than the standard 2-10-0; a resistance which was much more than could be attributed to the slightly greater weight of the Crosti. It was a complete mystery because the whole of the running gear, wheels, axles, coupling rods, etc were identical on the two engines, and the frames very nearly so. Furthermore, both of them had been built at Crewe. Possibly the difference was within the normal variation between two locomotives of the same class; and if so the advantage could have been the other way about, favouring the Crosti engine. Unfortunately, at that time, there was great difficulty in getting close agreement between the tests carried out on the Rugby plant and those conducted on the line; and this difficulty masked the difference in running resistance until it was revealed some time later. However the difference was there and it might also have been about 1% or 2%.[9]

A possible source of trouble in the tests was sooting up of the tubes in the Crosti preheater, because they did not get cleaned by the abrasion of solid particles in the flue gases, as did the boiler tubes, for virtually all these solid particles stayed in the front smokebox. This soot might have reduced the heat transmission. It might have been removed by fitting a soot blower or sand gun, as was often done on oil-burning locomotives. The Crosti preheater also suffered from the sulphur in the coal. The temperature of the exhaust gases was reduced below the dew point of sulphuric acid, and so this was deposited on the lower ends of the preheater tubes and the final smokebox and chimney. The preheater tubes were also liable to corrosion on the water side, which could probably have been countered by suitable water treatment. In view, however, of the test results the extra expenditure would have been hard to justify. It is true that the Crosti boiler was successful in Italy, but the conditions were entirely different. The price of coal was considerably greater, and the locomotives converted to the Crosti system were rebuilds of engines which were relatively old and of mediocre efficiency by modern standards.[10]

In 1958, after Riddles' retirement, R. C. Bond (the new Chief Mechanical Engineer) had three of the '9Fs' (Nos 92165, 92166, and 92167) fitted with the American Berkley mechanical stoker. All three engines had double chimneys. The reason for trying mechanical stokers was that brake tests (comparing vacuum and air brakes) had shown that if 50 or more loaded coal wagons were to be hauled at 60mph by one '9F' a combustion rate well beyond the capacity of hand-firing would be needed.

The history of mechanical stokers is interesting and somewhat inconclusive. The mechanical stoker was used first in the United States of America on locomotives having a grate area of some 60sq ft and burning an average of about two tons of coal per hour. By using a mechanical stoker it was possible to increase substantially the boiler evaporation rate and also the weight behind the tender, the latter by sometimes as much as 25%. As regards the consumption of coal, efficiency was lowered in respect of water evaporated per pound of coal at higher rates of working, but expense per ton/mile was less because of the better utilisation of the power of the engines. However, it was necessary to accept the inconvenience of having to cut the coal down to a size suitable for the stoker, and this could lead to the expulsion of cinders from the chimney and consequent loss. Apart from this disadvantage, the need to cut the coal to a suitable size was a major reason for the lack of enthusiasm in the United Kingdom for mechanical stokers.

It is interesting, however, to compare the experience of the French railways. The Nord Railway had encouraging results from fitting mechanical stokers to their 2-10-0 locomotives of the '5.1200' class. These engines had boilers identical with those of the famous Nord 'Super-Pacifics', with a narrow grate of only 38sq ft, and with carefully selected fuel they obtained boiler efficiencies comparable to those experienced with hand-firing on the same engines. French railways were, however fortunate in that the coal briquettes, so frequently used for fuel, were of a suitable size for the stoker.

André Chapelon decided on mechanical stokers for his famous '240P' class 4-8-0 express passenger locomotives. However, he made an important alteration to the firebox by lengthening the brick arch so that the small coal particles, which would have otherwise been ejected, would be burned. He found that the consumption of heat for the same steam production was only 10% more than that of his earlier '240.700' class 4-8-0s. (Both classes were, of course, rebuilds of the Paris-Orleans '4500' class Pacifics, with a grate area of 40.4sq ft.) One of the '240P' class, indeed, produced what is probably the finest steam locomotive performance on a power-to-weight basis ever recorded anywhere. No 240P5 hauled a 17-coach train, weighing 800 tons (including a dynamometer car) at an average speed of 66.3mph over the $19\frac{1}{2}$ miles between Les

Below: Diagram of the '9Fs' fitted with mechanical stokers.

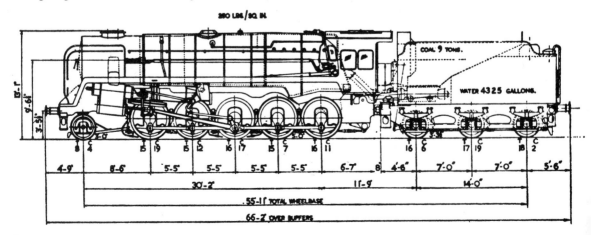

Laumes and Blaisy summit, the average rising gradient of which was 1 in 188. The last two kilometres, up 1 in 125, were covered at 61.2mph, with a recorded drawbar horsepower of 3,175, which corresponded to 3,600 at a uniform speed on the level. The pressure in the boiler was constant during the whole run and the water level in the gauge still stood at 6cm when the regulator was closed at the end of the effort. It is unlikely that such an outstanding performance could have been produced with hand firing.[11]

The type of mechanical stoker used by the Nord Railway and by Chapelon was the HT-1 pattern manufactured by the Société Stein et Roubaix.

In England the Berkley stoker on the '9Fs' gave disappointing results. Tests on the plant at Rugby showed that when the stoker was feeding coal at the maximum rate that the grate could burn, the efficiency of combustion was so much lower than the normal that the evaporation was no higher than the maximum short term rate with hand firing. But the stoker-fitted locomotive could maintain this rate continuously, and thus had greater potential capacity. Unfortunately the traffic people were unable to find regular services on which the power of these engines could be fully exploited.[12]

In 1948 Bulleid fitted the Berkley stoker to one of his 'Merchant Navy' class Pacifics. The experiment did not last long because any advantages were more than offset by disadvantages. As the feed screw in the tender could not cope with coal containing lumps larger than a 6in cube, the trials were conducted at Eastleigh motive power depot where the tub-loading coal stage enabled large lumps to be removed, though at the expense of time and labour. It could not have been done at depots with hopper coaling plants. In addition, the coal was crushed by the stoker to enable it to be blown into the firebox by steam

nozzles, and considerable amounts of half-burned particles were rejected through the chimney. This stuff blew back down the train, entering windows of compartments and covering restaurant car table cloths with smuts and burn marks. It was to prevent this sort of trouble, as we have noted, that Chapelon lengthened the brick arch.

The difference between the British and French results were so marked that there must be some suspicion that the Stein et Roubaix stoker, together with the lengthened brick arch, was much better than the Berkley. Certainly the statement expressed by E. S. Cox that hardly anywhere had the use of a mechanical stoker been justified for grate areas below 50sq ft must exclude France.[14] Nevertheless, the 40.2sq ft grate area of a Class 9F locomotive was within a fireman's ability to fire up to any rate of output required of it for the length of time needed on any service on BR, with the grades of coal that were still generally available. The mechanical stoker could probably have coped with coal of much lower quality, but it would then have used so much more coal that the reduction in price would not have lowered the total cost of the fuel consumed. Had a power output been required that a fireman could not have maintained for even relatively short periods, the mechanical stoker might still have been worthwhile; but there was no demand for such power. To work really well a mechanical stroker needs to be supplied with a graded coal, and the grading of coal leads to higher prices; but even at its best the stoker is needed only for large locomotives which are habitually worked hard.[15]

The third major modification applied to the '9F' 2-10-0 was the fitting of a Giesl ejector. This apparatus had been

Below: Giesel oblong ejector as fitted to '9F' No 92250.

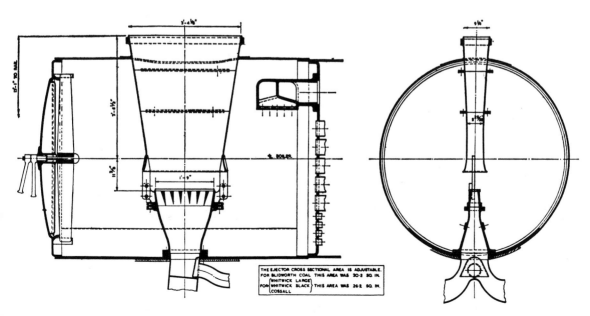

THE EJECTOR CROSS SECTIONAL AREA IS ADJUSTABLE.
FOR BLIDWORTH COAL THIS AREA WAS 30.2 SQ. IN.
(WHITWICK LARGE)
FOR (WHITWICK SLACK) THIS AREA WAS 26.2 SQ. IN.
(COSSALL)

invented by Dr Adolph Giesl-Gieslingen of Vienna, a steam locomotive engineer who had become particularly interested in draughting. Gieslingen appreciated that the diameter of the true ejector is small in relation to its total length, but to disperse the steam and gas of a large locomotive it would have to be far too long to fit any into loading gauge. He therefore decided to use a number of short true ejectors instead of one long one. Placed side by side and in parallel, they would have resulted in a long base with several disadvantages. Gieslingen got over this difficulty by fanning out seven exhaust nozzles along the centre line, so that effectively seven true ejectors were merged into one to form a chimney which was very narrow in width but long from front to rear. The practical objective of the device was the increase the draught on the fire and reduce the back pressure, so as to increase the power for a given coal consumption. It was claimed, too, that low grade coal (hitherto deemed unusable by locomotives) could be burnt economically.

The Giesl ejector had certainly improved considerably the performance of many types of locomotive in several countries; but Bond, as CME British Railways, had refused to try it because he was perfectly satisfied with the excellent draughting on Riddles' Standard locomotives. Nevertheless, because the Coal Board was anxious to find a market for low grade coals, pressure was brought to bear on him to try the apparatus. Reluctantly, Bond had one '9F', No 92250, fitted with a Giesl ejector and made arrangements to test it against a normal engine of the class. Dr Gieslingen approved the test conditions and attended a number of the tests himself. The broad results of the tests were that with the coal normally used and at average rates of working there was an increase in indicated horsepower of from 4.8% to 7.25% and a fuel saving of only 3.72%. The higher savings claimed were not realised and results with low grade coal gave no inducement to purchase at the price the Coal Board demanded.

The trouble was that the Coal Board's price structure made any attempt to use low grade coal hopelessly uneconomic. The Giesl ejector, adjusted so as to give the same maximum power output on test as the standard double chimney, did give a small economy thanks to the much reduced exhaust steam pressure when using the same grade of coal. It also enabled a good output to be obtained from an inferior variety of coal, when graded to a reasonable size, but at the expense of a higher consumption to an extent which outweighed the reduction in price. With the same inferior coal, but in the form of slack, the performance of the engine was lowered appreciably and it was too irregular for a proper standard of testing; furthermore, there was a still greater increase in consumption, again by far more than was compensated by the reduction in price. With a still lower grade of slack it was almost impossible to keep the engine going at all, and more unburnt coal reached the smokebox than was burnt.[16]

To cope with such grossly inferior coals it would have been necessary to redesign the whole firebox, grate, and ashpan; and this would probably have entailed turning the engine into a 2-10-2, with the penalty of a loss in adhesion in starting and heavy climbing.

The whole of this chapter shows how difficult it was to improve on the excellent original design. It may even be doubted whether the double chimney was worthwhile because it was extravagant on fuel except when the engine was working really hard.[17]

Notes

1 Information to the Author from R. A. Riddles and R. G. Jarvis
2 J. G. Jarvis, information to the Author
3 ibid
4 R. A. Riddles, information to the Author
5 Jarvis, op cit
6 P. N. Townend, information to the Author
7 D. R. Carling, information to the Author
8 ibid
9 ibid
10 ibid
11 A. Chapelon, information to the Author
12 R. C. Bond, *A Lifetime with Locomotives* (Cambridge, Goose & Son, 1975), pp248-9
13 Col H. C. B. Rogers, *Bulleid Pacifics at Work* (London, Ian Allan, 1980), p44
14 E. S. Cox, *Locomotive Panorama* Vol 2 (London, Ian Allan, 1966), p95
15 Carling, op cit
16 ibid
17 R. A. Riddles, comment to the Author

Left: No 92024, built at Crewe with a Crosti boiler. Note the chimney in front of the firebox. *British Railways*

Top: No 92021 with Crosti boiler in steam at Wellingborough. *Ian Allan Library*

Above: Crosti-boilered No 92022 at Wellingborough Midland Road station in August 1955. *A. W. Flowers*

Right: No 92026 with a Crosti boiler near Mill Hill in May 1957 with loaded hoppers for Wellingborough. *Brian Morrison*

Top left: No 92028 with Crosti boiler at Toton on 25 March 1956. *J. Buckingham*

Above left: No 92027 with a Crosti boiler on a freight train, giving a view of the unpleasant conditions on the footplate. *Ian Allan Library*

Left: An ex-Crosti '9F', No 92024 at Holbeck, showing the difference at the front end after removal of the preheater drum. *T. A. Greaves*

Above: Ex-Crosti No 92022 climbing to Ais Gill summit with an early morning freight train from Carlisle (Kingmoor) on 17 July 1965. *Maurice S. Burns*

Right: An unusual view of an ex-Crosti '9F' at Holbeck. *T. A. Greaves*

Above: The end of steam at Birkenhead, showing a number of '9Fs' (including an ex-Crosti) and one Class 5 4-6-0 on 28 August 1967. *J. L. McIvor*

Left: A typical Giesl ejector, similar to that fitted on No 92250 for trial. *Schoeller-Bleckmann*

Below: No 92250, the last '9F' built at Crewe, fitted with its Giesl ejector. *D. P. Williams*

Bottom: The result of trials with a Giesl ejector with poor coal. The pile of material in front of the wagon is from the smokebox of No 92250, together with a lesser amount from the grate and ashpan, after six hours running on the test plant. The few large clinkers contrasts with the vast amount of smokebox 'char'. *D. R. Carling*

Top left: Ex-Crosti No 92021 pulling out of the loop at Shap Summit on to the main line with a southbound freight train on 25 July 1964. *A. R. Thompson*

Left: Ex-Crosti No 92029 hauling a freight train near Penistone, GC, in the Sheffield Division in 1964. *T. A. Greaves*

6
From *Rocket* to *Evening Star*

Because Riddles' 2-10-0 locomotive for British Railways was the last of the very long line of steam engines to be designed and built in the country of their origin, it is perhaps appropriate to discuss the development history of the principal components and features which saw their ultimate issue in an engine which was equally at home on any kind of traffic from heavy freight to express passenger. It is difficult indeed to see how steam traction could have progressed very much further in its traditional form. The term 'traditional' refers to the arrangement of the steam locomotive embodied by George Stephenson in his *Rocket* of 1829 — an arrangement which has never been departed from successfully, but which has, of course, been vastly improved in whole and in detail by successive generations of locomotive engineers, building on the experience of the past. In the compass of one chapter it would be impossible to give more than a very general description of those developments which were principally responsible for the technical advance of the steam locomotive.

It is suggested that the four most important elements of a steam locomotive are the boiler (including the whole steam circuit), the valves and valve gear, the wheels, and the frames. Because development of these four elements did not by any means take place at the same time, they are considered separately in the following pages.

Boiler

For a description of the boiler of the *Rocket* one cannot do better than quote Nicholas Wood, who was a judge at the Rainhill trials of 1829 (noting that he ascribes the engine to Stephenson's son, Robert, who did of course supervise the building of the engine.)[1]

'The *Rocket* engine of Mr R. Stephenson ... differs from the locomotive engines previously described in this work, in the mode of raising steam. The boiler is cylindrical with flat ends, 6ft long and 3ft 4in diameter. To one end of the boiler is attached a square box, or furnace, 3ft long, by 2ft broad, and about 3ft deep; at the bottom of this box, the firebars are placed, and it is entirely surrounded by a casing except at the bottom, and on the side next the boiler, leaving a space of about 3in between this casing and the furnace, which space is kept continuously filled with water; a pipe on the underside communicating with the boiler, supplies it with water; and another pipe at the top allows the steam to pass off into the boiler. The upper half of the boiler is used as reservoir for steam the lower half being filled with water. Through the latter part of the boiler, copper tubes reach from one

end of the boiler to the other, being open to the firebox at one end, and to the chimney at the other. In the boiler of the *Rocket* there were 25 tubes, 3in in diameter. The cylinders were placed, one on each side of the boiler ... and worked one pair of wheels only; were 8in diameter, with a stroke of $16\frac{1}{2}$in; diameter of large wheels, 4ft $8\frac{1}{2}$in ... The principle of generating steam by this engine, is the *exhausting power of the chimney*, which is aided by the impulse of the steam from the cylinders, being thrown into the chimney by two pipes, one from each of the cylinders. The area of surface of water, exposed to the *radiant heat* of the fire, was 20sq ft, being that surrounding the fire-box or furnace; and the surface exposed to the heated air of flame from the furnace, or what we shall call *communication heat*, 117.8sq ft; the area of the grate bars being 6ft.'

This then was the brilliant conception that has been retained, basically unaltered, in conventional steam locomotives up till the present day; and it will be noted how closely the description of boiler heating surface, etc, agrees with that in current usage.

As compared with all the previous steam locomotives, Wood currently points out[2] that: 'The great improvement, however, was the increased evaporative powers of the engine, by the employment of numerous tubes of small dimensions; thus the *Rocket* engine, weighing only $4\frac{1}{4}$ton, had an extent of evaporative surface, $3\frac{1}{2}$ times greater than the old engines, weighing seven tons and upward ... These tubes were used at the suggestion of Mr Booth, treasurer to the Liverpool and Manchester Railway Company.'

Experience with the *Rocket* resulted almost immediately for an order, placed in 1829, for more of similar type. In these the Stephensons increased the number of boiler tubes to 88 but reduced their diameter to 2in. Whilst the boiler length and diameter remained the same, the heating surface was considerably increased. Two more engines were ordered early in 1830, but these embodied a very important improvement; for instead of the tubes terminating directly into a chimney with, of necessity, a very wide base, a smokebox was provided.

In August 1830 the Stephensons delivered the *Northumbrian* to the Liverpool & Manchester Railway; and this engine, the last of the 'Rocket' type, incorporated the last major development of the boiler. Instead of the firebox, as previously, being a separate construction, it now became an integral part of the boiler. A year after the Rainhill trials, therefore, George Stephenson and his son had produced the final form of the locomotive boiler.

The *Northumbrian* was followed two months later by the *Planet*, in which the Stephensons had taken another revolutionary step by removing the cylinders from their previous location outside and at the back of the boiler, to a position below the smokebox and inside the frames.

Mention must be made here of the steam dome, the presence or absence of which became quite a prominent feature of later designs. Its introduction was due to the difficulty which had been experienced in preventing priming on the very early engines, and the resulting carriage of water into the cylinders. Engines that followed the *Planet* in the 1830s and 1840s had a dome which was placed either on top of the firebox or on the boiler barrel. From the dome steam was collected by a steam pipe to the cylinders, the opening of which was governed by the driver's regulator in the cab.

Priming continued to be a problem and many varieties of domes were devised to prevent it. Some engineers, indeed, replaced the steam dome by a vaulted roof to the firebox casing to increase the steam space; others provided two domes, of which one, over the firebox was merely a steam vessel and the other, near the chimney, contained the regulator. The reason for placing the latter so far forward was to avoid a long steam pipe, which, with the joints and glands of the period, often caused leakage when the water level was high.

Until about 1839 it was the normal practice to clothe the boiler with strips of wood lagging, while the firebox casing was usually left bare. Later a layer of felt was placed beneath the wood strips; but in heavy rain water got between the strips and wet the felt. From about 1847, in consequence, the wood was replaced by a sheet iron covering over the felt.

Boiler fittings at this period included water level gauges, fusible plugs (to melt in the event of the water level dropping below the firebox crown, with danger of a boiler explosion), blow-off cock, and spring-loaded safety valves. Boiler pressure was low; in Daniel Gooch's early Great Western engines, for example, it was 50lb/sq in.

Gooch at first preferred the vaulted roof, or 'Gothic', type firebox and fitted it to his big 'single', *Great Western* with 8ft driving wheels. This was the prototype of the famous 'Iron Duke' class of 1846, probably the most successful express locomotives of the first half of the 19th century; but in these latter engines Gooch got the steam space for his domeless boilers in replacing the Gothic firebox by a raised firebox casing. The 'Iron Dukes' had the greatly increased boiler pressure of 100lb/sq in (later raised to 120), and the steam was taken by a perforated pipe which terminated at a regulator box in the smokebox.

A few years later Archibald Sturrock, a friend of Daniel Gooch and his Works Manager at Swindon, became Locomotive Superintendent of the Great Northern Railway, where he adopted a policy of large boilers with pressures up to 150lb/sq in. In a letter to E. L. Ahrons[3] he wrote: 'The success of the GWR was nearly entirely due to the introduction of fireboxes of about double the area of those used on the narrow gauge in 1850, and the raising of the steam pressure from 80 to 150lb ... Engines, like horses, go well in many shapes, sizes, and colours, but no variations such as position and diameter of a wheel or diameter of cylinder are worth anything unless there be plenty of steam *at a high pressure*, which gives economy by expansion. The finest gun is no use unless there be plenty of powder.' (the terminology reflects Sturrock's love of hunting and game shooting. By 'narrow gauge', Sturrock meant the standard gauge as compared with the Great Western's broad, or 7ft gauge.)

Although the early Stockton & Darlington Railway engines were coalburners, the vast majority of engines, during the first 30 years after the opening of the Liverpool & Manchester Railway, burnt coke. A clause in the Act for that railway prohibited the emission of smoke; but this requirement could not be met if the engines were fired with coal, owing to the small size of their fireboxes and the short boiler tubes. Some locomotive engineers devised elaborate fireboxes to deal with the problem and had various degrees of success. The Midland Railway found the solution in 1859 by introducing the simple firebox with brick arch and deflector plate, which is still the standard arrangement.

Another important invention of 1859 was Giffard's injector for introducing feed water into the boiler. It was adopted at once by all British railway companies. Previously feed pumps had been used, and many had the disadvantage that, being driven off the crosshead, they were unable to feed the boiler when the engine was stationary. Consequently, if the water level got low, the engine had to be run backwards and forwards along a siding.

When Patrick Stirling succeeded Sturrock as Locomotive Superintendent of the Great Northern Railway in 1866, he built engines which had domeless boilers, but without any raised firebox casing. However, he avoided the risk of priming by lowering the top of the inner firebox. This was a satisfactory system for normal working, but, because it reduced the circulation of water in the boiler, it was not an acceptable arrangement for engines that had to work particularly hard.

The first Belpaire fireboxes, with their characteristic flat-topped casings, to be made in Great Britain were turned out in 1872 by Beyer Peacock & Co for the Belgian Malines-Terneuzen Railway. The first British locomotives to have them were a class of 0-6-2T engines for the Manchester Sheffield & Lincolnshire Railway, built in 1891. The Belpaire firebox subsequently became standard on that railway and also on its successor, the Great Central Railway.

In September 1897 G. J. Churchward was appointed Chief Assistant Locomotive Superintendent of the Great Western Railway, clearly designated as the eventual successor to the increasingly infirm William Dean. One of his first actions was to cancel the raised round-top firebox, which had appeared on the drawings of the forthcoming 'Badminton' class 4-4-0 engines, and substitute a Belpaire firebox, to which he had been attracted by the direct system of staying. Next, amongst 20 more 'Duke' class 4-4-0s being built, *Bulldog* was given a boiler of greatly increased size and straight-sided and longer Belpaire firebox. *Bulldog* had a dome, but *Waterford*, completed three months after *Bulldog* and the last of the 'Badminton' class, had the same boiler without a dome. The reason for this was that Churchward had verified by experiment his belief that steam collected from the top of a flat firebox casing resulted in less priming that steam collected from a dome. To get adequate steam space in his domeless boiler, Churchward raised the firebox casing so that there was a depth of 2ft between it and the crown of the inner firebox.[4]

In February 1902, when Dean was still nominally Locomotive Superintendent, Swindon turned out the first engine built entirely to Churward's ideas, an express passenger 4-6-0 which was later named *William Dean*. It had a large diameter domeless parallel boiler and Belpaire firebox with raised firebox casing. It experienced some trouble, however, for there were broken stays and cracks at the junction of the boiler barrel and the firebox, which were traced to indifferent boiler circulation. To remedy the trouble, Churchward increased the size of the water legs of the firebox by curving the side plates and increasing the diameter of the boiler barrel at the firebox end by coning the upper part of the rear barrel plate, whilst leaving the lower part horizontal. The resulting sweep of the firebox ensured the success of the Churchward boiler. Churchward had, indeed, achieved his aim of a free flow to and from the firebox and free circulation, both for the rising steam and for the incoming feed water which took its place.[5]

Churchward's belief in the superiority of the Belpaire firebox was supported by a boiler explosion on a LNWR compound 0-8-0 in 1921, Though the explosion was due to a defective safety valve, it drew attention to the small volume above the inner firebox for the disengagement of steam on LNWR engines, and many of them were fitted with Belpaire fireboxes from 1923 onwards.[6]

On the other hand, Sir William Stanier's introduction of the Churchward domeless boiler on to the LMS was not successful. The LMS had a number of different types of water for its engines, some of which was softened, and the Churchward arrangement was inadequate to compete with the priming which occurred. Domes, in which the regulators were inserted, had therefore to be fitted.[7]

There was another development in boiler construction on which Churchward commented during a discussion of a paper on *American Locomotive Practice* read before the Institution of Locomotive Engineers. He said: 'Probably, to the English locomotive engineers, the part of the paper which deals with boilers is the most interesting; especially the reasonably wide firebox which the author has described. An express engine with a similar box has just been put on the Great Northern Railway by Mr Ivatt, and I trust it will have a good trial in England. I think English locomotive engineers are within a reasonable distance of adopting it, and I am sorry that the French Atlantic engine, which is to be put on the Great Western Railway is not fitted with it!'[8] In fact, the large boiler and wide round-topped firebox led to Ivatt's 'Atlantics' being so successful that these features were retained on all the succeeding Great Northern and London & North Eastern Pacific express locomotives. Churchward, too, built a Pacific, the famous *Great Bear* to try the wide firebox out for himself. The relative merits of the Belpaire and round-top fireboxes have been discussed in Chapter 3.

The most notable development at the end of the 19th century was, however, the introduction of superheating. In 1898 a 4-4-0 simple expansion engine with two outside cylinders, designed by Wilhelm Schmidt and built by Borsig, entered service on the Prussian State Railways. It was immediately apparent that something revolutionary had arrived on the railway, because the engine showed an economy over simple expansion engines using saturated steam of 30% in water and 20% in coal. A similar engine was shown two years later at the Paris Exhibition of 1900. This superheater was of the smokebox pattern, but Schmidt also designed the earliest superheater with elements housed in flue tubes, which was fitted for the first time by Flamme in 1901 on locomotives of the Belgian State Railways.

In England Sir John Aspinall had provided a smokebox superheater for one of his Lancashire & Yorkshire Railway Atlantic locomotives in 1899, and was sufficiently satisfied to equip five more of them in 1902. This superheater was housed within a chamber recessed into the boiler barrel immediately behind the smokebox. It would nowadays be considered rather as a steam dryer, but it was undoubtedly efficient.

In 1906 G. J. Churchward made his first trial of superheating by fitting a Schmidt fire-tube superheater to the Great Western Railway two-cylinder 4-6-0 No 2901 *Lady Superior,* and in the same year George Hughes of the Lancashire & Yorkshire Railway fitted two of that Railway's standard 0-6-0 goods engines with the same type. These were the first fire-tube superheaters to be used in the United Kingdom. The following year a Great Western four-cylinder 4-6-0 was provided with the American Cole superheater; and in 1908 Churchward produced his own Swindon pattern superheater, based on the Cole type, which was installed in another four-cylinder 4-6-0. In the same year the famous Great Western Pacific, *The Great Bear*, was turned out from Swindon, equipped with the Swindon No 1 Superheater.

Also in 1908, D. Earle Marsh of the London Brighton & South Coast Railway built his 'I3' class 4-4-2 express passenger tank engines with Schmidt superheaters. It is generally considered that the running of one of these locomotives in 1909 on the 'Sunny South Special' express over 77 miles of the London & North Western Railway main line between Rugby and Willesden, without having to stop for water, drew attention to the considerable savings to be effected by superheating. The LBSCR engine, No 23, worked this train, weighing some 250 tons, between Brighton and Rugby, in comparison on alternate days with the LNWR 'Precursor' class engine No 7 *Titan*. The performance, indeed, of No 23 led to the production on the LNWR of superheated versions of the 'Precursors' and their 4-6-0 contemporaries, the 'Experiments'. These were the 'King George the Fifth' and 'Prince of Wales' classes respectively. As mentioned in Chapter 1, however, the high superheat adopted, which facilitated the billiant performances of these two classes, was rather ahead of the lubrication that could be afforded by the oils available at the time.

By the time that W. A. (later Sir William) Stanier arrived on the LMS, suitable oil were becoming available for high superheat: nevertheless, Stanier brought with him the continued Great Western practice of low superheat. The LMS, however, were already using a three-row superheater on the 'Princes', 'Georges', and 'Claughtons', with a higher degree of superheat; and Stanier was persuaded, says Riddles, to fit three rows to his range of new engines, in order to reduce coal consumption. This was done with the desired effect. It was not, incidentally, until after nationalisation that three-row superheaters were fitted to the Great Western 'Kings', with consequent improvements to their performance.

Valves and Valve Gear

The *Rocket's* valve gear was primitive by later standards. The brass slide valves were actuated by two loose eccentrics. In reversing the engine the eccentric rods were lifted our of gear and reversed by hand. The eccentrics were actuated by drivers screwed into the axle. There was no attempt to use the expansive properties of steam, and indeed there was only one point of cut-off. Nevertheless, the advantage of expansive working had been appreciated by the Stephensons, for the 1828 there is the first recorded instance of an arrangement for this which was applied to the *Rocket's* predecessor, the 0-4-0 engine *Lancashire Witch*. Two French engineers gave a description of the method of expansive working, of which the following is an extract: 'On one of the axles is fixed a toothed bevel wheel which turns another bevel wheel placed horizontally and attached to a vertical shaft, which (passing through the boiler) operates a rotating plug valve: by means of this valve it is possible to obtain the expansive action of the steam during half the stroke of the piston . . . It appears that the two pipes which carry the steam to the steam chests unite in a vertical pipe in which the turning plug valve operates. There are two toothed quadrants which the engineman by a handle can turn at will through a quarter of a revolution about their centres; in their front position they permit the rotating valve to produce its effect by causing the steam to work by expansion, in the second position they prevent this and the steam acts only by the effect of its elasticity on its entry into the cylinder. Ordinarily the cut-off is operated at the beginning of the run in order to economise the steam when only a small quantity has been formed, and it is used without expansion when in full activity.'[9] J. G. H. Warren comments: 'We gather from this description that the plug valves operated by the bevel wheel on the axle must have rotated in sleeves having ports whose position relative to the steam passages to the cylinder could be altered by means of the quadrants.'

During the years following the building of the *Rocket* there were various steady improvements in the valve gear, but by 1840 there was as yet only one point of cut-off for the steam in the cylinder. Then, in 1841, Robert Stephenson, on a visit to Derby, said to the North Midland Railway locomotive superintendent: 'There is no occasion to try any further at scheming valve motions; one of our people has now hit upon a plan that beats all the other valve motions.'[10] The 'Stephenson Link Motion', to which this announcement referred, was indeed a dramatic invention and it had an incalculable effect on the future of the steam locomotive. The original idea seems to have been due to a young draughtsman, William Williams, employed by Robert Stephenson & Company. A patternmaker of the firm, William Howe, developed the idea into a practicable arrangement which was both ingenious and extremely simple. On the crank axle were two eccentrics for each cylinder, one governing forward movement and the other reverse. From each eccentric a rod ran forward to a short vertical link, the eccentric for forward running being connected to the top of the link and that for reverse running to the bottom of the link. The link was suspended from an arm on the reversing shaft, controlled from the cab. From top to bottom of the link there was a slot in which moved a slide block connected to the valve spindle. When the slide block was in the middle of the slot, no movement was imparted to the valve spindle. When, by an adjustment of the reversing shaft, the link was lowered, the slide block came under the control of the forward eccentric, which imparted the required movement to the valve spindle; and when the link was raised the eccentric for reverse running stook control. When the link was in the extreme bottom or top positions, the link was in full gear, either forward or backward; whilst in between mid and full gear, steam was cut off at various percentages of the link's travel and the steam was being used expansively.

The immediate result of the introduction of the link motion was considerable economy in fuel consumption through the introduction of variable and increased expansion, and distribution was so much improved that really high speed became feasible.[11]

Slide valves were used universally at the time of the introduction of Stephenson's link motion valve gear, and the advent of piston valves still lay far into the future. Up till the end of the century the slide valves of most engines had a travel of less than 4in in full gear and a lap of about 1in. As a result, if they were driven in the theoretically most economical way, with a fully opened regulator and a short cut-off (to make the maximum use of expansion), the valve travel was so short that valve ports were not opened sufficiently to allow free admission and exhaust for the steam, causing throttling and considerable back pressure in the cylinders. The normal method of working, therefore, was with a longer cut-off and partially opened regulator — a method which also caused some degree of throttling. Fuel consumption in either case was higher than it would have been with well-designed long travel valve gear. Locomotive engineers were aware that if valves were given longer laps and longer travel, wide open ports could be obtained with a short cut-off. But slide valves are very heavy and there was a reluctance to give them a long travel on account of the increased wear which followed the higher speed demanded for the valve to travel a longer distance in the same time.

The way to the improvement in the steam circuit in British locomotives was pointed by William Adams, Mechanical Engineer of the London & South Western Railway. In July 1891 a series of trials were carried out with one of his 'X2' class outside cylinder 4-4-0 express locomotives, No 582. Adams' engines were fitted with his ingenious 'Vortex' blast pipe. This had an outer annular orifice for steam and an inner circular funnel for the gases; the latter forming the upper portion of a bell-mounted scoop which was open to, and faced, the bottom rows of boiler tubes. This arrangement allowed the exhaust steam to be emitted at a lower velocity than with the ordinary blast pipe, and the area of its escape was so proportioned as to reduce the back pressure on the piston to a minimum. The reduction of the velocity resulted in a more uniform flow of air through the fire, so that no large cinders were expelled from the chimney.[12]

The eminent French locomotive engineer, André Chapelon, had a very high opinion of the Vortex blast pipe. He wrote:[13] 'A very remarkable exhaust, which perhaps attracted insufficient attention at the time, is the Vortex blast pipe, the Adams system of annular exhaust the fitting of which to London & South Western locomotives started in 1885, and with which more than 500 locomotives of this railway and many French locomotives of the Nord and Ouest Companies were eventually equipped.' Chapelon added that it answered the four main requirements of an exhaust: a low back pressure on the piston; a draught which was at such a level as to allow the pressure and water level to remain constant in the boiler; an automatic adjustment so that it was effective at all power outputs; and an action which allowed the fire to burn equally over the whole surface of the grate, resulting in the highest combustion efficiency. He concluded: 'The fouling of the annular blast pipe seems to have been the sole reason that this excellent arrangement was, rather prematurely moreover, abandoned.'

The trials with No 582 consisted of five runs with trains of different weights over the routes London-Bournemouth, Bournemouth-London, London-Exeter, Exeter-Woking, and London-Salisbury. A striking feature for the time was that the engine was driven with regulator fully open at speed and with a short cut-off. For instance, a cut-off of 17% was recorded at 68mph down 1 in 386, and at 78mph down 1 in 100. Even more striking was the low coal consumption. On the first run the coal used per ihp hour was 1.98lb. On the second run the maximum recorded was 2.39lb; whilst on the other three runs the figures were between these two. No 582 was burning Welsh coal similar to that used on the Great Western Railway.[14]

Although the trials were held in 1891, it was some years before the results were reported to the outside world. An account was eventually given in a paper presented to the Institute of Civil Engineers by Adams, in collaboration with his Locomotive Works Manager at Nine Elms, W. F. Pettigrew, and recorded in the proceedings of 1895-96. This paper was read shortly before Churchward became Works Manager at Swindon, and it is quite likely that he was amongst those listening to it; but if not he would undoubtedly have read it later. He knew, therefore, that it was possible, even with existing valve settings, to work with full regulator and short cut-off, with consequent low coal consumption. It would have been apparent to him that, as No 582 incorporated no other unusual features in its design, the result must have been due entirely to the Vortex blast pipe. At the same time, the published indicator diagrams showed the throttling that one would expect from the small port openings obtained by short valve travels at such a reduced cut-off.

It is conceivable that Churchward, pondering on these results, believed that they could be achieved with much less loss of power through the use of wide port openings and large diameter steam pipes to provide a good steam circuit from regulator to exhaust. Furthermore, with the advent of satisfactory piston valves, which had much less friction than slide valves, the objections to a long valve travel had largely disappeared. (There was the additional factor, which had apparently been largely overlooked in the past, that if an engine is habitually working at a very short cut-off, the long travel valve is actually travelling little further than a short travel valve at a longer cut-off.)

To get his wide port openings, Churchward increased the valve travel by over 50% of that normally used by nearly doubling the length of the valve laps. By these means the steam port opening and the expansion period were increased at all cut-offs, and a full exhaust opening was obtained over a longer period. The superiority of Churchward's design practice was convincingly demonstrated in the trials in 1925 between Great Western 'Castle' class 4-6-0s and London & North Eastern Pacifics of Gresley's first design; and long travel long lap valves were soon adopted by all locomotive engineers for engines equipped with piston valves. (The first successful piston valves were designed by W. M. Smith, Chief Draughtsman of the North Eastern Railway, in 1887[15]; but it was only slowly that they were widely taken into use.)

In 1884 a young Belgian engineer named Walschaerts invented a very successful valve gear — not long after, indeed, Stephenson's link motion; but it was some time before its advantages were appreciated in Great Britain, where the Stephenson gear satisfied all the requirements of engines with inside cylinders. In fact, it was not till the first decade of the 20th century that Walschaerts valve gear started to become popular, particularly for engines with outside cylinders. It had various advantages for it was very simple, it was light, everything was easily 'get-at-able', and no eccentrics were needed for an engine with two outside cylinders.

The motion of the valve was obtained from two independent movements. One of them was taken through links from the crosshead of the engine, giving a valve travel equal to the steam lap plus the lead (ie, the amount that the valve opens to admit steam before the piston reaches the limit of its stroke, to cushion the shock, and perhaps about $\frac{1}{16}$in) on either side of the central position. The remaining portion of the valve travel, which gave varying degrees of port opening, was derived from a return crank on the driving axle. The crosshead was connected to the bottom of a vertical combination lever, the upper end of which was connected to a radius rod. Between these two connections, but much closer to the latter, the valve spindle was connected to the combination lever. From the return crank a rod actuated a slotted expansion link which oscillated about a fixed trunnion. Inside the slot was sliding block attached to the rear end of the radius rod. This block was moved up and down in the slot by the reversing shaft and its position determined the direction of travel and the point of cut-off, in approximately the same manner as the Stephenson link.

The Walschaerts gear was fitted to the '9F' class and, indeed, all the engines designed by Riddles except for his three-cylinder Pacific *Duke of Gloucester* which had Caprotti poppet valve gear. Subsequently some of the Riddles Standard locomotives were given the Caprotti gear and, had steam continued, some of the '9Fs' might have had it too, for Riddles regarded poppet valves as the best in principle for steam locomotives.

Wheels

The size, number, and arrangement of the wheels of a steam locomotive are determined by the following factors:
  1 The length and weight of the engine,
  2 the axle load permitted on the lines over which it will have to work,
  3 the maximum speed at which it will have to work,
  4 the gradients and curves of the lines for which it is intended,
  5 the nature of the tasks for which it is required, and
  6 the weights of the trains that it will have to haul.

The *Rocket* had the simplest possible wheel arrangement for it had a single leading pair of driving wheels and a trailing carrying axle — a 0-2-2 in later terminology. The driving wheels were 4ft 8½in in diameter, which was the same, for some obscure reason, as the gauge of the Liverpool & Manchester Railway (the standard gauge at the present time). All the later 'Rocket' type had 5ft diameter driving wheels, as did the succeeding 'Planets', though these had the 2-2-0 wheel arrangement. All these engines were intended to work both passenger and goods traffic on the Liverpool & Manchester Railway. However, it was not long before the Stephensons discovered that single driving wheels had insufficient adhesion to work heavy goods trains. They therefore modified the 'Planet' type to produce an engine with four coupled wheels of 4ft 6in diameter — a 0-4-0. *Samson* and *Goliath* of this class were supplied to the Liverpool & Manchester in 1831 for heavy goods and banking work.

The next problem was axle load. The 5½ton on the driving wheels of the 'Planet' class were too much for the light fish-bellied rails of the Liverpool & Manchester. Stephenson decided therefore to add a third pair of wheels behind the firebox producing a 2-2-2. The addition of the trailing axle had the additional advantage of checking the pitching of the engine on the light track. The driving wheels were still Stephenson's standard 5ft.

The first 0-6-0 goods engine with inside cylinders was built by R. Stephenson & Co for the Leicester & Swannington Railway in 1834; the wheels having the 4ft 6in of the 'Samson' class.

By the latter 1830s the 2-2-2 had become the standard wheel arrangement for main line passenger engines on nearly all railways, with driving wheels of usually 5ft 6in diameter. In 1840, however, Stephenson's 'Mail' engines for the North Midland Railway had 6ft driving wheels. Engines running on the 7ft broad gauge of the Great Western Railway had much larger driving wheels.

Stephenson's *North Star* of 1838 had 7ft driving wheels (again, matching the gauge of the railway), as did Daniel Gooch's 'Firefly' class of 2-2-2s built from 1840. The era of big wheels to get higher speed had arrived. In the trials between the broad and narrow (ie standard) gauge, one of the 'Firefly' class, *Ixion*, ran from London to Didcot at an average speed of 47.5mph with a load of 81½ton, and 52.4mph with 61ton. On the return journeys, on the slightly falling gradients, the respective averages were 50mph and 54.6mph.

Large wheels, having apparently proved their worth, Daniel Gooch produced in 1847 his 4-2-2 'Iron Duke' class with driving wheels of 8ft diameter. The four leading wheels did not constitute a bogie, but were four rigid axles. But in 1849 Gooch adopted the bogie for his 4-4-0 saddle tank engines. These were intended for the heavily graded and sharply curved routes of the South Devon Railway, but they worked the majority of the passenger trains from Newton Abbot to, eventually, Penzance until the end of the broad gauge.

A great advance in passenger locomotives, but rather before its time, was Sturrock's 4-2-2 bogie express passenger locomotive of 1853, with 7ft 6in driving wheels to work the Scotch expresses over the Great Northern main line.

By 1852 most of the leading railways were building 2-4-0 passenger engines with inside cylinders for the more difficult routes and also to work heavy trains, demanding greater adhesion than the 'singles' could supply. Nevertheless, many locomotive engineers preferred single driving wheels for the fastest running, believing that coupling the wheels hampered speed. There were probably grounds for this belief in the days when softer metal could lead to uneven tyre wear, and thus to coupled wheels of slightly different diameter.

Bogies come into greater use during 1860-65, and 4-4-0 engines appeared, for instance, on the sharply curved Pennine and Whitby routes of the Stockton & Darlington and North Eastern Railways respectively. Of these early bogies, by far the most notable was that designed by W. Adams in 1865 for his 4-4-0 North London Railway tank engines. It was a great advance on any previously produced and was the first to be provided with lateral traverse for the pivot. Adams used the same type for his London & South Western Railway 4-4-0 express passenger engines.

In 1863 Archibald Sturrock, in his search for greater power and adhesion, fitted a Great Northern Railway 0-6-0 goods engine with a steam tender which had all its wheels coupled and driven by cylinders supplied with steam from the engine's boiler. After satisfactory tests, a great number of similar engines were constructed. They proved capable of hauling heavy coal trains between Doncaster and London via Lincoln; but the boiler was being asked to do too much and coal consumption was heavy. In addition, they were far from popular the enginemen, who considered that they were being charged with looking after two engines instead of one.

Adhesion in goods engines was enhanced when in 1864-66 outside cylinder 0-8-0 tank engines were built by the Avonside Engine Company for the Vale of Neath and

Great Northern Railways; and these eight-coupled locomotives were the most powerful tank engines in the country, as well as being the first examples of eight-coupled wheels in the United Kingdom.

In 1878 the leading pony truck made its first appearance in this country when 15 2-6-0 goods engines were built to the designs of W. Adams for the Great Eastern Railway. They were not one of Adams' most successful designs, but their indifferent performance was not due to any deficiency in the pony truck.

It was not till 1889 that eight-coupled tank engines were followed by 0-8-0 tender engines, when the Barry Railway acquired some with this wheel arrangement built by Sharp Stewart for the Swedish and Norwegian Railway.

In 1894 David Jones designed and built for the Highland Railway the first 4-6-0 engines in Great Britain. These were the famous locomotives which, though theoretically goods engines with their 5ft 3in coupled wheels, were used for both heavy goods and passenger trains over the Highland main line between Perth and Inverness. In their success in this dual role they might be considered as precursors of the '9Fs'.

Churchward's 4-6-0s eventually had the de Glehn pattern bogie, fitted to the French Atlantics purchased by the Great Western Railway. This bogie proved so good that it was adopted in due course, first by the Southern Railway, then by the LMS, and ultimately by British Railways. It was probably the de Glehn bogie on the LMS Pacific that saved the 'Coronation Scot' train from disaster as it approached Crewe at the end of its successful attempt on the world speed record for steam; when the train was switched over sharp reversed curves to No 3 platform while still travelling at 50mph. A Gresley 'A4' class Pacific would probably have crashed because the LNER bogie, as then fitted to them, caused excessive rolling at high speed. Subsequently Gresley asked Stanier for drawings of the LMS bogie and adopted its system of side checks.[16]

Churchward never designed an engine with unguided coupled wheels, and he led British locomotive engineers in his widespread use of the two-wheeled pony truck for heavy freight, mixed traffic, and tank engines. Churchward's example was soon followed by J. G. Robinson of the Great Central Railway on his 2-8-0 heavy goods engines of 1911 and by the then H. N. Gresley on his 2-6-0 and 2-8-0 mixed traffic and goods locomotives from 1912 onwards.

Gresley's 'V2' class 2-6-2s showed that the use of pony trucks instead of bogies constituted no bar to high speeds, and his subsequent 'Cock o' the North' class 2-8-2s were the only British express locomotives to rely on pony trucks for guidance. But these otherwise fine engines were spoiled by their rigid coupled wheelbase. The curving route of the Edinburgh-Aberdeen main line (for which they had been specifically designed) led, not only to continual trouble with hot axleboxes on the coupled wheels, but to side pressure spreading the track. This trouble would not have occurred with the flexible wheelbase that Riddles designed for his 2-10-0s.

The first British engine with 10-coupled wheels was the three-cylinder 0-10-0 tank engine designed by J. Holden in 1902 for the heavy suburban traffic of the Great Eastern Railway. It was intended to prove that the rapid acceleration of electric trains could be equalled by steam, to counter a proposal to electrify the GER suburban network. The electrical engineers said that a train of 315 tons could be accelerated to 30mph in 30sec from the start. Holden's *Decapod* accelerated a train of 355ton to 30mph in approximately that time, and proposals for electrification were dropped. However, the engine was too heavy, and its long wheel base too rigid, for the track, so it was rebuilt as a 0-8-0 tender engine.

Chapelon's work on 'internal streamlining' and the opening up of the steam circuit had a profound effect on more than boiler design. The removal of throttling and consequent easy steam flow conferred such a freedom of movement that the diameter of the coupled wheels no longer had the same restriction on the speed with which they could rotate. Speeds of 100mph were easily obtainable with the 6ft 2in wheels of the Southern Pacifics, and it is conceivable that the '9Fs', with their 5ft wheels could also have reached these heights, in the light of the ease with which they surpassed 90mph.

Frames

The frames of a locomotive obviously constitute one of its most important elements because they provide the foundation upon which the whole thing is built. The *Rocket* had bar frames, as did two engines sent by Stephensons to America in 1829. But, whereas bar frames subsequently became standard practice in America, they were soon abandoned in the United Kingdom. The earlier engines of the 'Rocket' type also had bar frames, but the *Northumbrian* of 1830 had a combination of bar and plate frames, whilst the succeeding 'Planet' class had outside plate frames. These formed a complete rectangle, and were made of wood, bound at the corners with iron plates and angles. There were, in addition, four intermediate wooden frames, the principle function of which was to support the crank axle in the event of breakage, but they also carried the slide bars. These inside frames were really stays with bearings for the driving axle. Stephenson's six-wheeled (2-2-2) *Patentee* of 1833 had outside sandwich frames and also four inner frames. The outside sandwich framing originated by Stephenson was adopted by Daniel Gooch for both broad and standard gauge engines of the Great Western Railway, and it was used until 1865. Sandwich frames were continued again on the GWR from 1872, and a large number of standard gauge engines were so built until 1891 when this framing was finally abandoned. The sandwich originally consisted of ash between two metal plates, but later the Great Western and a number of private builders employed oak. This latter wood, though strong and durable, had the disadvantage that the bolts securing the flitch plates to the timber tended to work loose and the acid in the oak caused the bolts to corrode. From 1886 to 1891, therefore, teak, which is an oily wood, was substituted and this proved satisfactory.

Sandwich frames were utilised by the Great Western long after other companies had abandoned them because on the longitudinal road of the broad gauge the engines with sandwich frames ran much more smoothly and with less vibration than those with solid plate frames.[17]

When Stephenson, in 1841, introduced his long boiler engines with all wheels in front of the firebox, he discarded outside sandwich frames in favour of inside plate frames made of $\frac{3}{4}$in thick iron plates. Inside plate frames became eventually, of course, the normal standard for British designed engines.

Alone amongst British manufacturers, the firm of Bury Curtiss & Kennedy continued using bar frames until about 1850. From about 1846 mixed frames became popular for 2-2-2 engines, with outside plate frames and bearings for the carrying wheels and inside plate frames and bearings for the driving wheels. An early example of entirely outside frames was provided by J. E. McConnell's large singles for the London & North Western Railway. They were built to meet the intention announced in 1852 of running express trains between London and Birmingham in two hours. They might well have been able to do this if the permanent way had been suitable, but the attempt was never, apparently, made.

During the second half of the 19th century examples of the various types of frame mentioned above, together with other combinations, were in common use; but by 1900 inside plate frames were almost universal for new construction, except on the Great Western where outside plate frames were still prevalent in the latter days of steam.

Over the years fracture of frames has presented an all too frequent a problem. They have to be strong and rigid enough to withstand the thrust imposed on them by the power of the engine, yet flexible enough to traverse with ease the curves of the routes over which they are intended to run. There is an interesting example from France of these somewhat conflicting requirements. The main lines of the old Est and PLM Railways follow, in general, the valleys of the great rivers, and are consequently routed in long sweeping curves. These companies, therefore, generally built their locomotives with frames thin enough to flex to the curves. Furthermore, because their gradients were mostly long but not severe, short periods of high power working were not required. The Nord and Paris-Orleans, on the other hand, generally cut across the valleys, with a number of short steep climbs and consequent difficult starts from many of their stations. Their locomotives, therefore, were built with thick and very rigid frames to stand up to the frequent heavy demands for power. In trials conducted over the Nord main line with trains worked by Nord Pacifics, Chapelon's rebuilt PO Pacifics, and 4-8-2s from the PLM and Est, two out of three of the Est engines fractured their frames.

General

As stated at the start of this chapter, there were, of course, many other factors that played a considerable part in the evolution of the steam locomotive, such as brakes, springs, safety valves, ash pans, self-cleaning smokeboxes, and countless others; but these, important as they were, constituted, merely, the necessary ancillaries for the perfection of the whole. What is remarkable, indeed, is that in some 130 years of steam locomotive development there has been no revolutionary departure from the original Stephenson concept, and if one compares the replica of the *Rocket* with the preserved *Evening Star*, the first and the last of the line, it is comparatively easy to follow the development between the two.

Notes

1 Nicholas Wood, *A Practical Treatise on Rail-Roads*, 3rd Edn (London, Longman, 1838), pp324-6
2 ibid, pp331-2
3 E. L. Ahrons, *The British Steam Railway Locomotive 1825-1925* (London, Locomotive Publishing Co, 1927), pp93-4
4 Col H. C. B. Rogers, *G. J. Churchward: A Locomotive Biography* (London, George Allen & Unwin, 1975), pp78-80
5 ibid, p97
6 E. S. Cox, *Locomotive Panorama*, Vol 1 (London, Ian Allan 1966), p23
7 ibid, p104
8 Rogers, op cit, p124
9 J. G. H. Warren, *A Century of Locomotive Building by Robert Stephenson & Co 1823-1923* (Newcastle upon Tyne, Andrew Reid, 1923), p147
10 ibid, p363
11 W. F. Pettigrew, *A Manual of Locomotive Engineering*, 2nd Edn, Rev (London, Charles Griffin, 1901), pp 149-150
12 ibid, pp232-3
13 André Chapelon, *La Locomotive a Vapeur, 2nd Edn, Vol 1 (Paris, J. B. Baillière et Fils, 1952), pp132-3 (Author's tr)*
14 Pettigrew, op cit, pp288-313
15 Ahrons, op cit, p287
16 Col H. C. B. Rogers, *Thompson & Peppercorn: Locomotive Engineers* (London, Ian Allan, 1979), p51
17 Ahrons, op cit, p47

Top: Patrick Stirling's GNR eight-foot bogie single No 22, with a domeless boiler and without raised firebox casing. *Ian Allan Library*

Above: GWR 'Duke' class 4-4-0 No 3272 *Amyas*, as originally built with round top firebox and outside plate frames. *British Railways*

Right: Dean's raised firebox casing on his 'Achilles' class 4-2-2 express engine, shown at Swindon at the head of the 10.30am express from Paddington to Torquay on 26 June 1898. *British Railways*

Top: The ultimate development of the Dean/Churchward 'Bulldog' class — No 3434 with domeless tapered boiler and shaped Belpaire firebox, and with outside plate frames. *British Railways*

Above: One of Churchward's famous 'City' class express locomotives, No 3433 *City of Bath*, derived from the Dean/Churchward type 4-4-0s, and showing the same features (though with larger coupled wheels) as the 'Bulldog' class. One of these engines, *City of Truro*, was the first steam locomotive to exceed 100mph. *British Railways*

Centre left: The first of Ivatt's large Atlantics for the Great Northern Railway, No 251, showing the wide round-top firebox. This famous engine is now preserved at the National Railway Museum. *T. G. Hepburn*

Left: A Marsh 'I3' class superheated 4-4-2 tank engine, No 21, on a London Brighton & South Coast Railway Pullman car express; a sister engine of No 23 which competed with the LNWR on the haulage of the 'Sunny South Special'. *Ian Allan Library*

103

Left: One of the first bogie engines. A South Devon Railway 4-4-0ST, *Lance*, built in 1851. It is working the first broad gauge passenger train on the West Cornwall Railway into Redruth station in 1867.
British Railways

Centre left: SDR 'Leopard' class 4-4-0ST engine *Stag*, built in 1872. This wheel arrangement was so successful that the SDR 4-4-0Ts practically monopolised passenger services west of Newton Abbot until almost the end of the broad gauge. *Stag* and her sister *Leopard* were the last broad gauge engines in steam, being employed in shunting surplus broad carriage stock at Swindon after broad gauge services had ceased.
British Railways

Below: Churchward's use of the pony truck; a GWR '43xx' class 2-6-0 locomotive No 4321. *British Railways*

Top right: A Churchward Atlantic, No 183, built as such to compete with the French Atlantics (from which were copied the de Glehn bogie).
British Railways

Right: The first 4-6-0 type in Great Britain; No 104 of David Jones's 'Goods' locomotives of 1894 for the Highland Railway. *Ian Allan Library*

Below right: No 2001 *Cock o' the North*; the first British express engine to rely on a pony truck for guidance.
National Railway Museum

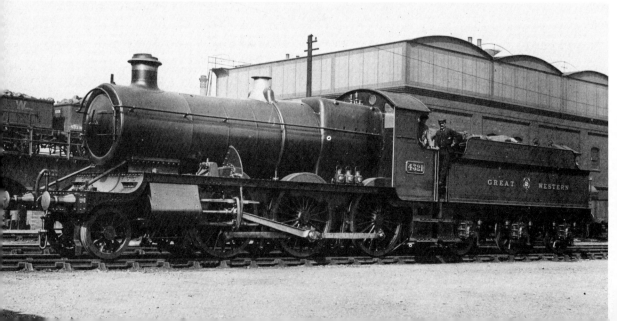

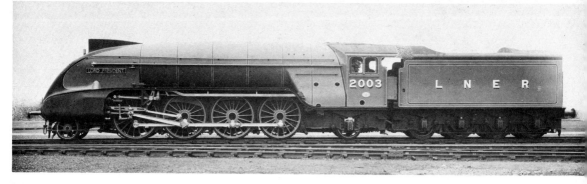

Above: Gresley's 2-8-2 express locomotives in their final form; No 2003 *Lord President.   Modern Transport*

Right: The first British engine with 10 coupled wheels; Holden's Great Eastern Railway 0-10-0 tank engine No 20 *Decapod.   Ian Allan Library*

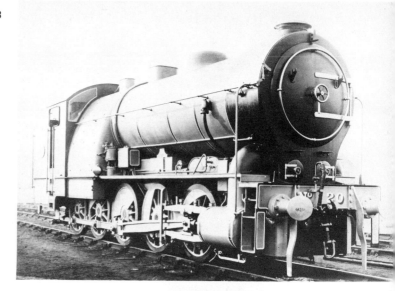

Below: The end of it all — No 92220 *Evening Star* at the Institute of Mechanical Engineers centenary celebrations.   *T. A. Greaves*

Appendix

Summary of numbers and dates

BR No	Date Built	With-drawn	BR No	Date Built	With-drawn	BR No	Date Built	With-drawn
92000	1/54	7/65	92059	10/55	9/66	92119	1/57	9/67
92001	1/54	1/67	92060	11/55	10/66	92120	2/57	7/67
92002	1/54	11/67	92061	11/55	9/66	92121	2/57	7/67
92003	1/54	3/65	92062	11/55	6/66	92122	2/57	11/67
92004	1/54	3/68	92063	11/55	11/66	92123	3/57	10/67
92005	2/54	8/65	92064	12/55	11/66	92124	3/57	12/66
92006	2/54	4/67	92065	12/55	4/67	92125	3/57	12/67
92007	2/54	12/65	92066	12/55	5/65	92126	3/57	8/67
92008	3/54	10/67	92067	12/55	11/66	92127	4/57	8/67
92009	3/54	3/68	92068	12/55	1/66	92128	4/57	11/67
92010	5/54	4/66	92069	12/55	5/68	92129	4/57	6/67
92011	5/54	11/67	92070	1/56	11/67	92130	4/57	5/66
92012	5/54	10/67	92071	1/56	11/67	92131	5/57	9/67
92013	5/54	9/66	92072	2/56	1/66	92132	5/57	10/67
92014	5/54	10/67	92073	2/56	11/67	92133	6/57	7/67
92015	9/54	4/67	92074	2/56	4/67	92134	6/57	12/66
92016	10/54	10/67	92075	3/56	9/66	92135	6/57	6/67
92017	10/54	12/67	92076	3/56	2/67	92136	7/57	10/66
92018	10/54	4/67	92077	3/56	6/68	92137	7/57	9/67
92019	10/54	6/67	92078	3/56	5/67	92138	7/57	7/67
92020	5/55	10/67	92079	4/56	11/67	92139	7/57	9/67
92021	5/55	11/67	92080	4/56	5/67	92140	7/57	4/65
92022	5/55	11/67	92081	5/56	2/66	92141	12/57	12/65
92023	5/55	11/67	92082	5/56	11/67	92142	7/57	2/65
92024	6/55	11/67	92083	5/56	2/67	92143	8/57	2/65
92025	6/55	11/67	92084	5/56	11/67	92144	8/57	12/65
92026	6/55	11/67	92085	6/56	12/66	92145	8/57	2/66
92027	7/55	8/67	92086	6/56	11/67	92146	9/57	4/66
92028	7/55	10/66	92087	8/56	2/67	92147	9/57	4/65
92029	7/55	11/67	92088	10/56	4/68	92148	9/57	12/65
92030	11/54	2/67	92089	9/56	2/67	92149	10/57	6/65
92031	11/54	1/67	92090	11/56	5/67	92150	10/57	4/67
92032	11/54	4/67	92091	11/56	5/68	92151	10/57	4/67
92033	11/54	9/65	92092	12/56	10/66	92152	10/57	11/67
92034	12/54	5/64	92093	1/57	9/67	92153	10/57	1/68
92035	12/54	2/66	92094	2/57	5/68	92154	10/57	7/67
92036	12/54	12/64	92095	3/57	9/66	92155	11/57	11/66
92037	12/54	2/65	92096	4/57	2/67	92156	11/57	7/67
92038	12/54	4/65	92097	6/56	10/66	92157	11/57	8/67
92039	12/54	10/65	92098	7/56	7/66	92158	11/57	7/66
92040	12/54	8/65	92099	7/56	9/66	92159	11/57	7/67
92041	12/54	8/65	92100	8/56	5/67	92160	11/57	6/68
92041	12/54	8/65	92101	8/56	10/67	92161	12/57	12/66
92042	1/55	12/65	92102	8/56	11/67	92162	12/57	11/67
92043	1/55	7/66	92103	8/56	5/67	92163	4/58	11/67
92044	1/55	4/65	92104	8/56	2/67	92164	4/58	7/66
92045	2/55	9/67	92105	9/56	1/67	92165	4/58	3/68
92046	2/55	10/67	92106	9/56	7/67	92166	5/58	11/67
92047	2/55	11/67	92107	9/56	2/67	92167	5/58	6/68
92048	2/55	9/67	92108	10/56	11/67	92168	12/57	6/65
92049	3/55	11/67	92109	10/56	11/67	92169	12/57	5/64
92050	9/55	9/67	92110	10/56	12/67	92170	12/57	5/64
92051	9/55	10/67	92111	11/56	10/67	92171	2/58	5/64
92052	9/55	8/67	92112	11/56	11/67	92172	1/58	4/66
92053	9/55	2/66	92113	11/56	10/67	92173	2/58	3/66
92054	9/55	5/68	92114	11/56	7/67	92174	2/58	12/65
92055	9/55	12/67	92115	12/56	2/66	92175	2/58	5/64
92056	10/55	11/67	92116	12/56	11/66	92176	3/58	5/64
92057	10/55	10/65	92117	12/56	12/67	92177	3/58	5/64
92058	10/55	11/67	92118	12/56	5/68	92178	9/57	10/65

Details of No 92196

Above: Double chimney '9F' No 92196 on exhibition at Noel Park on the occasion of the 750th Anniversary of Wood Green Borough Charter. Note the magnificent finish of the engine and the striking detail of the Walschaerts valve gear. *P. N. Townend*

Right: No 92196 with the smokebox door open. This photograph gives a fine view of the Walschaerts valve gear on the left hand side of the engine. *P. N. Townend*

Below: No 92196 showing the corresponding position of the valve motion on the right hand side of the engine. *P. N. Townend*

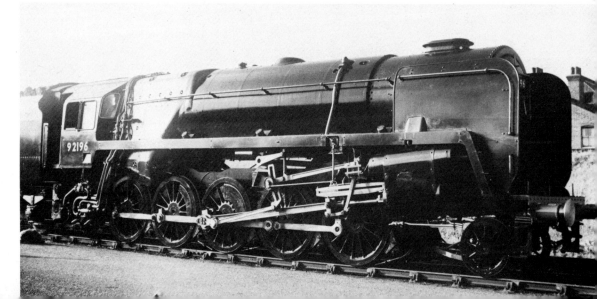

Above: No 92196 showing the copper pipes polished by Townend's charge hand fitter. This photograph also gives a good view of a '9F' tender.
P. N. Townend

Left: A good view of No 92196's flangeless centre coupled wheels and reversing shaft at Noel Park.
P. N. Townend

Below left: No 92196, showing the front of the engine. *P. N. Townend*

BR No	Date Built	Withdrawn
92179	10/57	11/65
92180	11/57	4/65
92181	11/57	2/65
92182	12/57	4/66
92183	12/57	4/66
92184	1/58	2/65
92185	1/58	2/65
92186	1/58	8/65
92187	2/58	2/65
92188	2/58	2/65
92189	3/58	12/65
92190	3/58	10/65
92191	4/58	12/65
92192	5/58	2/65
92193	5/58	6/65
92194	6/58	12/65
92195	6/58	5/65
92196	8/58	12/64
92197	9/58	9/65
92198	10/58	8/64
92199	10/58	8/64
92200	11/58	10/65
92201	12/58	3/66
92202	12/58	12/65
92203	4/59	11/67
92204	4/59	12/67
92205	5/59	6/67
92206	5/59	5/67
92207	6/59	12/64
92208	6/59	10/67
92209	6/59	12/65
92210	8/59	11/64
92211	9/59	5/67
92212	9/59	1/68
92213	10/59	11/66
92214	10/59	8/65
92215	11/59	6/67
92216	12/59	10/65
92217	12/59	7/66
92218	1/60	5/68
92219	1/60	8/65
92220	3/60	3/65*
92221	5/58	5/65
92222	6/58	3/65
92223	6/58	4/68
92224	6/58	9/67
92225	6/58	7/65
92226	6/58	9/65
92227	7/58	11/67
92228	7/58	1/67
92229	7/58	11/64
92230	8/58	12/65
92231	8/58	11/66
92232	8/58	12/64
92233	8/58	2/68
92234	8/58	11/67
92235	8/58	11/65
92236	9/58	4/65
92237	9/58	9/65
92238	9/58	9/65
92239	9/58	11/66
92240	10/58	8/65
92241	10/58	7/65
92242	10/58	5/65
92243	10/58	12/65
92244	10/58	12/65
92245	11/58	12/64
92246	11/58	12/65
92247	12/58	10/66
92248	12/58	5/65
92249	12/58	5/68
92250	12/58	12/65

* Evening Star

Building Details

92000-14 built at Crewe order No E487
92015-19 built at Crewe order No E491
92020-29 built at Crewe order No E488
92030-49 built at Crewe order No E489
92050-86 built at Crewe order No E490
92087-96 built at Swindon Lot No 421
92097-134 built at Crewe order No E493
92135-177 built at Crewe order No E494
92178-202 built at Swindon Lot No 422
92203-220 built at Swindon Lot No 429
92221-250 built at Crew order No E497

Notes

92020-29 fitted with Crosti boilers
92156-67 fitted with mechanical stokers
92250 fitted with Giesl ejector and chimney
92000/1/6/79 ⎫
92165/6/7/78 ⎬ fitted with double chimney
92183-92249 ⎭

Preserved locomotives

92134 on the North Yorkshire Moors Railway
92203 on the East Somerset Railway, named *Black Prince*
92212 on the Great Central Railway
92214 on the Peak Railway
92220 owned by the National Railway Museum, Yo
92240 on the Bluebell Railway

Below: The Riddles footplate used on all stand engines was designed to allow drivers a comfortable seat; and to group all controls to enable him to operate them without having to stand up. Note the reversing wheel turned at r angles to ease strain. This mock up was made put on exhibition at Marylebone where inspec and drivers were invited to express their opinio and to obtain their co-operation for the new p *R. A. Riddles*

Index